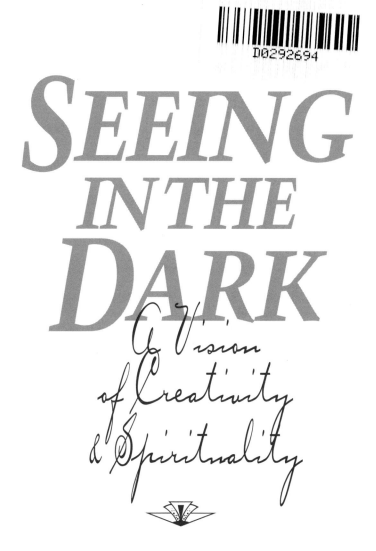

SEEING IN THE DARK

A Vision of Creativity & Spirituality

BEVERLY J. SHAMANA

ABINGDON PRESS / Nashville

SEEING IN THE DARK: A VISION OF CREATIVITY AND SPIRITUALITY
By Beverly J. Shamana

Copyright © 2001 by Beverly J. Shamana

This book is printed on acid-free paper.

Library of Congress Cataloging-in-Publication Data

Shamana, Beverly J. (Beverly Jean), 1939-
    Seeing in the dark : a vision of creativity & spirituality / Beverly J.
    Shamana.
    p.cm.
    ISBN 0-687-09106-3 (alk. paper)
    1. Creative ability—Religious aspects—Methodist Church. 2. Spiritual
    life—Methodist Church. I. Title.

BX8349.C74 S43 2001
248.4'87—dc21

                                                              00-045130

01 02 03 04 05 06 07 08 09 10—1 2 3 4 5 6 7 8 9 10

MANUFACTURED IN THE UNITED STATES OF AMERICA.

SEEING IN THE DARK

*T*his book is dedicated to

* Beginners who think they're all thumbs and want to befriend their inner artist

* Established artists who want to find deeper wells of the spirit for their creativity

* Creative people who need a boost

* My mother, Charlene Martin, role model and prolific collage artist who nurtured the creative seed in her children at an early age

* My departed father, Sylvester Martin, a creative plastering contractor and my cheerleader, whose voice I still hear from the great cloud of witnesses

Contents

Preface

*T*his book is about nostalgia, about coming home. It is not meant to teach you something you do not already know. Rather my intent is to recall what is already in your unconscious memory, placed there at the beginning of Creation. A modern sage has said that we know more than we know we know.[1] This wisdom is at the crux of these writings. My purpose is to remind you of what is scribbled on the inner cavity of your bones.

As you read these words, you are already creative. It comes as a gracious gift from God. You do not have to go someplace to learn it; and although it may be enhanced with training and practice, you breathe it with every breath you inhale. Creativity permeates the universe; ours is to recognize and express it for the glory of God, our inner joy, and the making of a world that honors the image of Christ.

The seed for this book began in 1982 with a snippet of a dream that came while I lived in the parsonage of my first church appointment. The dream offered a glorious and splendid light that shone through a window, piercing my writing pad like a prism. In the dream I placed my pencil on a three-pronged soap dish in the bathroom. Although I've pondered its meaning for many years, the original insight remains the same. Over time I've come to know that I am to use the tools of paper and pencil to scrub down to the under layer of things and make visible what is hidden.

Four years ago I was inspired by Julia Cameron's book, *The Artist's Way: A Spiritual Path to Higher Creativity*,[2] to form a covenant group of lay and clergy artists to read her book together and to explore the bond between faith and the arts. I was convinced the connection was there, but it seemed hidden. Two years into our meetings, we offered workshops at the annual conference. One hundred sixty persons came to talk about creative gifts as a pathway to God. Since then I have led many workshops and retreats in churches and other settings to continue the dialogue and to invite others to see what is hidden—the creative gifts within them and a wider spectrum of all our creative gifts from God.

SEEING IN THE DARK grew out of these workshops and the hunger to find affirmation for what is a natural expression of God's grace within us that I encountered. The articles and activities in the appendixes will offer some creative ways to start and to continue both your reading of the book and your discovery of your own creativity. I commend them to you. My prayer is that you will discover depths of your gifts that are waiting to bring you great joy, contribute to our world, and witness for Christ. Welcome home.

CHAPTER 1

The Hand Print of God

f you have ever watched an artist at work and said, "Some people have all the talent, and then there's me," or entertained thoughts such as, *I'm too old to be creative*, or *My seventh grade teacher said I shouldn't sing*, or *My brother has all the talent in our family*, then this book is for you. The myth that only certain kinds of people are creative—writers, composers, actors, painters, and sculptors—keeps many people from discovering their very own birthright to God's gift of creativity.

Are you among those who are neglecting or diminishing your creative expression because you are too busy or "just not good enough"? Finley Eversole, in *The Politics of Creativity*, writes, "In our society, at the age of five, 90 percent of the population measures 'high creativity.' By the age of seven, the figure has dropped to 10 percent. And the percentage of adults with high creativity is only two percent!"[1]

Somehow we have bought into the notion that our creative contribution must measure up to the standards set by someone else: grade school teachers, famous artists, parents, or popular figures of our time. We thereby allow our divine worth to become captive and imprisoned, thus diminishing our true potential. But, what if creativity is no respecter of age, place, culture, gender, skill, or experience? What if creativity is not something to be searched for but rather a sacred presence that flows through our veins naturally, like our blood? What if God sees to it that we are endowed with this precious attribute at birth? What if creativity is already there, just waiting to be used?

Our creative capacities are gloriously affirmed in the first six words of the Bible. "In the beginning when God created..." (Genesis 1:1), and again in verse 27: "So God created humankind in his image, / in the image of God he created them."

We know these words so well that often we rush past the mystery of creating and take for granted the divine connection between us human beings and God our Creator. Look at the creative principles at work in God's sacred process:

* to make something out of nothing;
* to bring order out of chaos;
* to select and combine elements to form something new;
* to bring light out of darkness;
* to bring life where none existed.

The "Divine Spark"

We are the offspring of a creative God whose hand print is stamped indelibly on our soul, marking us for continuing creativity in the world. This holy birthmark is the Creator's personal gift to the universe for all time. "The master has provided the spark," says French poet, Paul Valéry. "It is your job to make something out of it."[2] One day, after a creativity class, one of my students said in wonder and excitement, "I want to go out and dunk my hands into a bucket of clay!" I knew what he was feeling.

Though he wasn't a potter, his whole being reached for a tangible connection to the divine spark that had been awakened in him. He was ready to go and make something out of it. The hand print of God was upon his soul.

The imprint of God's hand does open us to new explorations and exciting discoveries. One of those surprising "aha's!" is that the creative muse does not conform to a schedule, appear upon demand, speak our language, or stay within our grasp (buckets of clay notwithstanding). The mystery of creating is that it meanders along at its own pace and settles in its own space, in spite of our attempts to control it. In making something out of it we find that this muse makes something new out of us as we learn to listen and attend, to prepare the way, then to move out of the way. In this way the answers and images can flow through us, sometimes swirling in and around us like water at low tide, resting where it will.

Baa, Baa, Black Sheep

This settling of creativity happened in my own life recently as I wrestled with a problem that seemed to yield no answer. I awoke one morning with a children's rhyme suspended behind my eyelids. As I lay in the dark, emerging from the mist of dream time, I let my eyes remain closed and wondered what this child's tune had to tell me. Several minutes passed. I tried to recall all of the words that I sang so many years ago. They returned slowly, line upon line, rhyme upon rhyme.

Baa, Baa, black sheep, have you any wool?
Yes sir, yes sir, three bags full.
One for my master and one for my dame.
One for the little boy who lives down the lane.
Baa, Baa, black sheep, have you any wool?

I opened my eyes. If we pay attention to our holy visitations, our dream-time companions, even the short snippets, we gain insight into the shape and fabric of our lives. During the day my dream teacher came and sat beside me to illumine the deep truths that were beyond my waking consciousness. I began to see with new eyes the value of the black sheep and its offering of self as its precious gift. The little sheep has nothing to say about who or what it is, or whether it will have any wool. It all comes with "sheephood," and it is all good.

The nursery rhyme continued to unfold its mystery to me in the abundance of the sheep's offering and usefulness. The little black creature has enough curly wool to supply the household and to give away to a neighbor child, who doesn't get the leftovers but the same quantity and quality of wool as the adult portion. It all comes from the black sheep, the misfit in the fold, the one labeled "outsider." I had not thought of that little rhyme in many years, but its reappearance taught me that we already know with a child's simplicity the abundance of God's gifts to each of us. And even those who are thought to be lacking any contribution of worth will have enough to give away generously in the gracious economy of God.

We already know the abundance of God's gifts to each of us.

14

Yes, I Can

Our creativity is likewise plentiful and valuable. We may have endorsed the "not me," "not yet," "not good enough" litany; but it is not too late to recover the simple insights of kindergarten, as Robert Fulghum suggests in *All I Really Need to Know I Learned in Kindergergarten*,[3] and allow the sacred gift of high creativity to flow freely through our grown-up veins once again as it did in childhood.

A church member named Margaret took my Creativity and Faith seminar in California. She confessed that she had never made any kind of presentation to adults in her entire life, though she had been asked many times. Margaret's passion is gardens. She carries a camera wherever she goes so she can take snapshots of gardens that catch her fancy. After the seminar Margaret was asked to present a program to a women's group in the church. In place of her usual "No, I can't," she gathered up her new courage and her blossoming self-discovery to present a wonderful slide show on "Gardens I Have Known" that is still remembered fondly.

At times we find ourselves stuck in our belief that our interests and our abilities are too small to make a difference for God or to touch another life. Meister Eckhart, the thirteenth-century mystic, said, "The outward work will never be puny if the inward work is great." Margaret experienced the hand print of God that freed her to share with friends the joy of her discoveries that had been locked away in secret. Creativity is a pathway to God, to the world, and to love of self. We give back to God when we walk that pathway to love the world in return.

15

The insight of potter Mary C. Richards rings true: "Every person is a special kind of artist and every activity is a special art."[4] Human beings are created for the transcendent; to engage in those things that lift the human spirit to its fullest potential. The words of Paul elevate us to this high calling in Philippians 4:8— "Finally, beloved, whatever is true, whatever is honorable, whatever is just, whatever is pure, whatever is pleasing, whatever is commendable, if there is any excellence and if there is anything worthy of praise, think about these things."

Reflections and Activities

1. Take a moment and think back over the past week. List one or more ways where you saw the creative principles of God in your life

✳ make something out of nothing _____

✳ bring order out of chaos _____

✳ select and combine elements to form something

  new _____

✳ bring light out of darkness _____

✳ bring life where none existed _____

Ponder your written reflections. Did you censor yourself? What would you add without the critic in your head holding you back? Is there a wide variety of activities on your list? Were you personally involved in the creative principles?

2. Each of us has our own unique brand of creative expression that contributes to the larger picture. Be sensitive to the ways God speaks to you about your creativity. Begin recording your dreams. Now that you have begun to be more alert to God's hand print, you will see it in more places.

3. In some cultures the symbol of the hand means healing and strength. You have begun a journey to heal your creative capacities and to open your hands to let the power of God's creativity flow through you.

✳ Find a bucket of clay! (You know the rest.)

✳ Keep a journal of creative revelations for one week.

✳ Draw a small hand on your daily calendar each time you feel or see the divine hand of God.

✳ Write a prayer of thanksgiving. Keep it with you in a special place.

CHAPTER 2

Healing the Past

*I*n the West African language of the Ashante people, the word *Sankofa*, has deep meaning. The colloquial translation is "Go back to fetch it." The symbol for Sankofa is a heart embellished with two scrolled circles that meet in the center. The Ashante of Ghana know it as a bridge word that honors the wisdom in learning from the past, especially their ancestors, in building the future. The concept of Sankofa is useful for us as we travel along our creative journey.

Each of us has footsteps behind us that are not our own. A careful look over our shoulder will bring into focus the persons who recognized and nurtured the growth of creative seeds planted within us. For these people who called forth our talents in many and different ways we owe a debt of gratitude. Like our family tree, they are the rich soil in which our creativity tree is planted. Another backward glance may also show us footprints we associate with pain that has wounded and hindered our creative growth. Our perseverance in spite of obstacles is a testament to courage, but the scars that remain can cause indelible marks and retard the full expression of our gifts.

The good news of the Sankofa principle is in the promise of restoring our creative imagination as the past meets the future within our embellished hearts. The healing of old wounds liberates us to experience the full joy of our gifts without the weight of the past that debilitates our creative energies. We can enjoy these gifts of God for our own sheer pleasure and for making a difference in the world around us.

There are many avenues of healing available to us when we are ready to move toward them. Maya Angelou shows us the healing power that comes from linking hands across the Sankofa bridge with our ancestors, who, like hers, trod in the dirt of history. In her poem *Still I Rise*, we feel their inner strength to overcome the crippling pain of many generations. They offer us encouragement to draw on our inner resources for the healing journey that we too may rise with the certainty of moons, suns, and tides for our dreams of tomorrow.

> You may write me down in history
> With your bitter, twisted lies,
> You may trod me in the very dirt
> But still, like dust, I'll rise.
> Just like moons and like suns,
> With the certainty of tides,
> Just like hopes springing high,
> Still I rise.
> Out of the huts of history's shame
> I rise
> Up from a past that's rooted in pain
> I rise...........
> Bringing the gifts that my ancestors gave,
> I am the dream and the hope of the slave.
> I rise
> I rise
> I rise.*

*From AND STILL I RISE by Maya Angelou. Copyright © 1978 by Maya Angelou. Reprinted by permission of Random House, Inc.

19

The spirit of Sankofa bids us to honor and listen to our ancestors, our oldest selves, for insight, for healing, for the impetus to begin a new future.

From Scabs to Jewels

A friend shared a treasured dream. She dreamed that she stumbled over a loose metal plate in a church walkway and scarred her ankle very badly. When she tried to apply bandages and wrappings to her wound, the scab had turned to jewels and sparkled as a patch of bright mosaic colors. My friend and I talked into the wee hours about the wounds we carry in our bodies and call ugly but are truly like precious gems of insight that lie beneath and upon the surface of our skin. Unsightly wounds and injuries are potent sources for healing and teaching.

The Courage to Look Back

The healing of our creative past requires the courage to look backward. Do you remember the creative exuberance of your childhood or youth? Many adults are unable to cherish these early memories because they are linked with the crusted wounds of rejection, criticism, and disillusionment. What happened to that child who could draw or tinker for hours, compose and sing songs, dramatize her day with spontaneity and satisfaction in the process and the product? That child is still with us, waiting to embellish our adult heart when we look back and trust the wisdom of Sankofa.

During an Advent series on Creativity and

Spirituality, John, a member of the church and a successful civil engineer, shared his longing to find the little boy inside him who loved to draw. "I used to be quite an artist," he said, speaking with a childlike innocence. "In school the teacher used my artwork as examples in the classroom. I mean, I really had talent. My grandmother agreed too." Then John's tone took on an adult manner. "Soon after I left grade school I was discouraged from continuing my art and put into 'the boy stuff.' You know, courses that would pay off later in a more lucrative career choice. My art was diverted by my well-meaning family and teachers. I think they just wanted the best for me." John now has a secure job in a company with upward mobility and a family of his own, but he misses the art. He didn't have to say any more. We all felt the hole in his soul.

In my seminars and workshops, I've seen the deep longing in the eyes of adults who struggle to recapture the natural creative expression and curiosity of their childhood that literally poured from their cells without boundaries or self-censorship. Somewhere between six years old and forty-six they lost the wonder and joy-filled desire that motivates us to follow our creative dreams. Pablo Picasso said, "Every child is an artist. The problem is how to remain an artist once you grow up."[1] To fulfill the essence of his humanity John needed something more than job security and stock options. At the close of our session, we prayed that John would ponder in his heart the gifts of the Advent season and rekindle his boyhood passion. He promised he would buy some paints and shuffle his schedule to include

Every child is an artist. The problem is how to remain an artist once you grow up.

21

the art of his soul. Now a dad himself, John is committed to nourishing art in his three talented children.

The Courage to Look Ahead

John is not alone in setting aside a creative hunger at an early age that now nibbles at his heels as an adult. The sorrow for lost creativity and lost opportunity can be overwhelming and stifle the yearning of our heart. The urge to cover our pain with layers of bandages can be overwhelming.

If we but continue to walk along the path with companions of compassion, as the travelers on the road to Emmaus, our eyes will ultimately be opened to the Christ who walks with us. Theirs was an ordinary road that led to the place of sacrament. There they recognized Jesus in their midst, bringing new life to those burdened with despair.

The meeting place for our Advent study series began as an ordinary room, a little-used third-grade classroom converted for our adult use. It too was made sacred by the anointing oil of prayer, laughter, Scripture, compassion, and care. As we walked the path of each person's story, we discovered our secret hurts and applied a healing balm. The Christ of Emmaus walks with us across the wounds of our past and leads us to a horizon illumined by hope.

The wisdom of Manitongquat says, "Life is the Sacred Mystery singing to itself, dancing to its drum, telling tales, improvising, playing and we are all that Spirit, our stories all but one cosmic story that we are love indeed."[2] Our pre-Christmas study group found the God who loves art through the telling of our sacred life stories. Each story became an essential plank in the Sankofa bridge as we shook hands with the past and welcomed a different future.

Awakening From Disappointment

The story of another Sankofa traveler unfolded on a Sunday afternoon in February. Lucille was strolling through the outdoor exhibit when we met at a Los Angeles church art show celebrating Black History Month. Like John, Lucille's wound was also connected to her childhood. She had basked in the praise she received from her family and friends as a young person. Lucille spoke in wistful tones as she described her adolescent ability in art. "I could look at anything and draw it," she said. "When I was eleven years old I entered a community drawing contest. I did very well and the judges chose my picture as the winning entry. But when they learned how young I was, they disqualified me because the judges did not believe that a kid my age could draw that well. They thought I had cheated, and I was never given the prize. After that I stopped drawing altogether. Now I just doodle in book margins when I'm on the telephone."

The artistic ability of this mature woman had been locked away many years ago, and the key to set it free had not been found. Like many of us whose search for our own creative soul is fragile and uncertain, we applaud others' works but participate from a safe distance. Lucille did not seem to be aware of her search for the key to open the door to her own lost art, but the poignancy in her voice betrayed her "I'm OK" demeanor. Like many others who are searching without knowing why, Lucille found her own creative juices stimulated by the vitality and pride of the exhibit and was transported back to the point of her childhood pain. The injustice done to her creativity was too great to overcome as a child, but now, on this cloudless February day, she seemed about to awaken, as if from a long winter's nap.

We walked among the vast array of images, drawing deeply from the wellspring of our cultural legacy with pride in our heritage. When we parted, Lucille patted her heart with a gentle gesture that seemed to say, "Be still my soul." I thought I heard the door to her past creak open, and I rejoiced with the ancestors in my heart. I doubt that I will ever see Lucille again, but her story will speak to my spirit for a very long time. Why? Because these are Spirit stories—journeys and events that God uses to heal our wounds and remind us of our connection to each other through the labyrinth of our lives. We are the storytellers of God with the power to heal and restore another's life by what we share. Mary Oliver says,

We are the storytellers of God with the power to heal and restore another's life by what we share.

"Whoever you are, no matter how lonely,
the world offers itself to your imagination,
calls to you like the wild geese, harsh and exciting—
over and over announcing your place
in the family of things."*

*Grateful acknowledgment is made for permission to use 5 lines from "Wild Geese," from DREAM WORK, by Mary Oliver. Copyright © 1986 by Mary Oliver. Used by permission of Grove/Atlantic, Inc.

Lucille reminds us that the wounds of our artistic past are not magically closed overnight, but the promise of their healing is very real. The ancient ones—the elders of the past and our cloud of witnesses—are the "amen corner" that pray for us and apply the splint to our souls and the curative balm to our confidence. They cheer us on and celebrate the restoration of our creative abundance that God has promised in Christ Jesus: "I came that they may have life, and have it abundantly" (John 10:10).

The Wellspring of Support

This wellspring of support has been gathered up by songwriter Dorie Ellzey in the chorus from one of her original songs:

> And the ones who've gone before us
>   will show us the way.
> And the ones who follow after will
>   welcome the new day.
> And the ones who've gone before us
>   will join in the chorus
> When we do, when we make it through.[3]

The healing of our creative past requires cleansing and affirmation from within and beyond ourselves to restore to us the depth of our unconditional worth. The following verses from Psalm 8:3-5 assure us of our infinite worth and join our humanity with the creative nature of God. Speak them aloud to encircle and heal any part of your wounded imagination.

"When I look at your heavens, the work of your fingers,
   the moon and the stars that you have established,

what are human beings that you are mindful of them,
  mortals that you care for them?
Yet you have made them a little lower than God,
  and crowned them with glory and honor."

The Whisper of Unquiet Desires

It is no accident that our yearnings to be creative are
divine and persistent. They are not meant to dry up
and blow away like dust even when they are left dormant for many years. Rather, these unfulfilled desires
appear again and again, like silent apparitions, unan-
nounced and uninvited at various stages and crises in
our life. They appear in dreams, during illnesses, in
our relationships, with our children, on our jobs, in
the dark and in the dawn, whispering to our soul that
they are not dead.

The hand of God has woven these creative yearnings into the fabric of the universe. They speak our
name from the margins of our doodle pads and the
perimeters of our lives, sketching the lines of our
ancestral kinship, waiting for full recognition.

When we do not know the richness contained in
Sankofa, we may mistakenly call it ancestral worship.
Rather its true and tribal meaning embraces familiarity
with and respect for the learnings of the past that still
live in our hearts through the teachings of the elders
who have preceded us. Wisdom that comes to us from
a source that predates rational cognition is embraced by
Clarissa Pinkola Estés, who counsels us in *Women
Who Run With the Wolves* that these unquiet desires
are known in the soul of our oldest self; in the "two-
million-year-old woman [who] will come visit you from
the night land. Perhaps she will be bearing the solu-

tion, or will show you that the answer is under your bed, or in your pocket, in a book, or behind your ear."[4]

The Ritual of the "Kitchen Cabinet"

When we feel that our creative voices have grown silent, let's gift ourselves with the time to walk across the bridge of Sankofa and seek the wisdom of our elders. To carry this conversation, let us listen to the voices of our past, our present, and our future. Let us invite the voices of the wise ones to join us in the ritual of the "kitchen cabinet." We do this by bringing—actually imagining—those we need to hear to our kitchen table or other gathering place. In this atmosphere of creative listening, we gather what we know of these special elders and open ourselves to how they might speak to our spirit and we then listen to their spirit stories. As we "hear," these words might be spoken or sung or chanted to bring about action, peace, healing, discernment, or other qualities needed at the time.

This ritual is made more graphic when each place has a name card or other characteristic associated with the voice. This mutual interchange makes tangible and visual the natural practice that happens in our head all the time. Sculptor Tim Holmes says, "I believe that all of us have inner characters that dramatically influence our daily lives."[5] We claim our own power and accelerate our healing when we are intentional about who speaks to us from the "kitchen table" of our soul. The words of Jesus remind us that we speak from what has been stored inside of us: "For out of the abundance of the heart the mouth speaks" (Matthew 12:34). It is from this abundance that we are filled with new spirit and are liberated to act. How often have we said, "I hear this voice in my head telling me to...." Taking charge and choosing which voices we listen to strips away the peeling paper of our old interior "kitchen walls" and readies them for a fresh décor, open to new, creative patterns and designs.

A Creative Kick in the Pants

Roger von Oech helps us choose our kitchen cabinet and the roles they might play. His book on creativity, *A Kick in the Seat of the Pants*,[6] shakes loose our inner voices and gives them a favored place in the creative process. Von Oech suggests four roles or types of thinking in the creative process: the explorer, the artist, the judge, and the warrior. Each has something unique to offer for our healing and continued growth.

The explorer helps us search for the materials with which to make new ideas. The artist is our imaginative, playful friend who takes the materials the explorer has collected and transforms them into original new ideas. The judge is our evaluative friend who examines what the artist has created and then decides what to do with it: implement it, modify it, or discard it. The warrior is our "doer" friend whose role is to take the ideas the judge has deemed worthy and do what's necessary to implement them. So who's coming to dinner at your kitchen table? Any or all of these friends have a valuable place in our creative journey.

Wounded Healers

The wounds and scars of our arrested creative heart may have begun as small acts, tiny words, almost like drops of water. If ignored, left to heal on their own, or covered with temporary salve, they grow from a hairline crack to a deep gully that diverts our gifts and drowns our very spirit—our faith. Henri Nouwen reminds us in his little book of immense depth, that we are all wounded healers. This may sound like bad news on first hearing, but the good news follows right behind. Our pains and wounds are the occasions God uses for a new vision. "The wound which causes us to suffer now," says Nouwen in *The Wounded Healer*, "will be revealed to us later as the place where God intimated his new creation."[7] This good news invites us to listen to the voices of our healing, thereby making peace with the wounds of the past, converting them to blessings for the new realm and reign of God that has already begun to break in upon us.

A Chinook blessing litany echoes the voices of the cloud of witnesses that walk the Sankofa bridge with us:

"We call upon all those who have lived on this earth, our ancestors and our friends, who dreamed the best for future generations, and upon whose lives our lives are built, and with thanksgiving, we call upon them to
"Teach us, and show us the way."[8]

Reflections and Activities

1. Nurture or nourish your Creativity Tree. This is a picture of the deep roots that nourish you today. Who belongs on the branches of this tree? in the roots? on the leaves? Write in the names on the roots and branches of the tree on page 163.

2. Create your Healing Mosaic. Use the image of the wound as a healing mosaic. Find inexpensive colored stones or tiles and make a small patch to remind you of your healing. Attach them to a sheet of cardboard or paper. Give it a name as a reminder of the jewels hidden in your wounds.

3. Jesus said we are blessed when we pray for those who persecute us. If you are finding it hard to hear God's voice or your own voice among the critics in your life that stifle your creative urges, they can be quieted with prayer. Right now, take a sheet of paper and sketch a large head in the middle of the sheet, profile or front view. Use at least three-quarters of the paper. Now begin to draw, in any manner you choose, the voices you hear.

✳ How many inner voices did you draw?

✳ What do you notice about them?

✳ Are there any surprises? confirmations?

✳ What is their prevailing message?

✳ How does the total picture make you feel?

✳ Is it the right size? How should it be changed?

✳ Where does this picture need to hang?

　　After reflecting on these questions, take a moment to invite God to bless the mess in your head. Place your hands on your collage of inner voices. Close your eyes. Recall the face of each voice in your picture. Offer a short prayer as you move from voice to voice.

"Loving God, I speak this prayer for (name of person). May your spirit enable (person) to affirm your creative gifts within me. Help me to use these gifts in the face of resistance if I must, but without anger. I pray that (person) may know that our creativity is a blessing to bring honor and praise to you. Amen."

4. Mark each step of your healing with a symbolic gesture: Ask a tree for a leaf; paint it. Find a special stone; dry and frame a flower; eat exotic fruit; go to a movie; put a lighted candle in a container of water; write or sing a song of affirmation; read healing Scripture.

5. List your "kitchen cabinet" and the qualities they represent. Make a place card for each. Put them in a sacred place and listen to what they might say to your questions, doubts, and deep yearnings.

CHAPTER 3

God Calls an Artist: The Bezalel Factor

If ever there was a Scripture aimed at blessing our creative gifts and the vocational calling of the artist within us, it is in the Old Testament Book of Exodus. There we meet Bezalel, who guided the building of the Tabernacle. Bezalel is the answer to the age-old question, "Where is art in the Bible? Is it worthy of God's attention?" Maybe you've never asked, but many people in our congregations know they were born to be creative but do not have the blessed assurance or the liberating certainty that God loves art and has shown through Scripture the rightness of following this call.

Meet Bezalel, Master Craftsman

Bezalel is not a household name in the Judeo-Christian tradition as is Paul, Sarah, or even Hur, Bezalel's grandfather and, according to the historian Josephus, the husband of Miriam. But within the Jewish tradition Bezalel is held up as the biblical model for the arts with the premier art museum in Jerusalem still bearing his name today. It is no small matter that the designation of this master artist was given to Moses on Mount Sinai, the place where he received the Ten Commandments and the laws and ordinances that governed every phase of Hebrew life. At this extraordinary meeting with God, the work of the artist was called into being. Here God named and empowered Bezalel of Judah for the task of constructing God's dwelling place among the people. A tabernacle would be built by artists. Moses tells the people of God's sacred assignment from the mountain:

"Then Moses said to the Israelites: See, the LORD has called by name Bezalel son of Uri son of Hur, of the tribe of Judah; he has filled him with divine spirit, with skill, intelligence, and knowledge in every kind of craft, to devise artistic designs, to work in gold, silver, and bronze, in cutting stones for setting, and in carving wood, in every kind of craft. And he has inspired him to teach, both him and Oholiab son of Ahisamach, of the tribe of Dan. He has filled them with skill to do every kind of work done by an artisan or by a designer or by an embroiderer in blue, purple, and crimson yarns, and in fine linen, or by a weaver—by any sort of artisan or skilled designer" (Exodus 35:30-35).

Bezalel's calling places the vocation of the artist in a historical context with a sacred beginning. Many artists in the church today are confused about their gift and wonder if it has any lasting value to the church. They question whether art is found anywhere in the Bible and how it can be used as a pathway to know God. Bezalel's assignment should put these questions to rest.

Putting Our Call to Work

Vocation comes from the Latin word *vocare* and means "to call," the work we are called to by God. In his book *Wishful Thinking,* Frederick Buechner describes our true calling as the place God calls us where our "deep gladness and the world's deep hunger meet."[1] This divine intersection is the place where God called and empowered Bezalel to use his gifts on behalf of God's people then and for future generations. "I have filled him with my power. I have given him understanding, skill, and ability for every kind of artistic work" (Exodus 31:3, TEV).

The first work among the community that follows Bezalel's call is the building of the Tabernacle, God's home among the people. This earthly dwelling is imagined as a structure of unmatched artistic beauty and function, something only an artist could envision and bring to completion. The specifications are dictated to Moses on Mount Sinai. The application of the details and the artistic license, however, remain with the builders who cut and polish the stones; carve the furnishings; sew the curtains; embroider the linens; and carry out the merger of design, skill, and artistry the structure requires. This ability to participate in God's own creative work is a further sign that we have inherited the desire to create beauty for pure aesthetic enjoyment and for functional use through the labor of our own hands. God's creative activity continues to unfold in the world around us through our creative gifts.

We have inherited the desire to create beauty for pure aesthetic enjoyment and for functional use through the labor of our own hands.

It is on Mount Sinai that we hear of Bezalel for the first time. We might surmise that his artistic skill was already known among the people of Israel and perhaps among other peoples. Let's imagine for a moment what this artist might have been doing before God chose him for the Tabernacle enterprise. Surely he wasn't just sitting around whittling sticks. The description of his qualifications for this divine commission suggests that he was not tapped with a magic wand from Mount Sinai, but he had developed and honed his skills long before he was named.

Perhaps he had worked on adorning the pyramids or other royal structures. Was he married? Can artists sustain a family and be creative too? Is there time to do both things well? How does an artist prepare for a job of this magnitude when it is not posted in the Help Wanted ads? We can only surmise that his practice and perfecting of methods and techniques prepared him to accept his lot confidently when tapped for the job.

Bezalel is a model for artists today. The time spent in discovering and refining our craft is not wasted time. It might be called *creos* time. Like *kairos* time, creos is time of a spiritual nature, a time of probing, of discovering the nature of our gifts, of testing the potential and scope of their application, of considering the ramifications for the long haul. Creos is a time of peaks and valleys, of undulating movement that we must learn to read, just as we read the hands of the clock in *chronos* time. Creos has a different rhythm that is measured by heartbeats and soul beats that tick at their own rubato pace—sometimes fast, sometimes slow, often in unmetered rhythms until we are aesthetically and spiritually satisfied.

> The time spent in discovering and refining our craft is not wasted time.

Ignorance of creos time is injurious to our spirit. We may learn too late that we have misread the possibilities and preparation of our gifts and overlooked the opportunities for serving God's call. If we could look behind Bezalel the artist, we might intuit that his readiness came through the honing of his craft, but also by the power that came from God who "filled him with divine spirit...," as Moses reported in Exodus 35:31. The divine synchronicity of God's timing and our artistic preparation frees us to say yes with integrity and deep gladness when God's expansive vision calls forth our gifts for holy service in places that exceed our limited view.

Our vocation, that which nurtures the Spirit of God within us, may not be our current work or activity. The figure of Bezalel, however, can inspire us to an unswerving trust in God, giving our best to whatever we are doing and preparing ourselves for God's horizon that calls forth our particular talents.

The Source of Vocation

During the interim, the writer who saw the Tabernacle as "a sketch and shadow of the heavenly one" has a message of hope. "Do not, therefore, abandon that confidence of yours; it brings a great reward. For you need endurance, so that when you have done the will of God, you may receive what was promised" (Hebrews 8:5; 10:35-36).

When God is the source of our vocation, the true meaning of our call is revealed. *Source* comes from the Latin *surgere*, meaning "to rise, to spring up, the starting point of a stream, as a spring, a fountain; the origin, that from which something comes into existence, develops, or derives." The origin of our call is God our Creator—the spring of our joy, the starting point of our true self, the fountain of our creativity, the *surgere* of all we are and hope to be. A modern-day philosopher, Michael Polanzi, has said that we know more than we know we know. This deep knowing taps into the current of collective voices where Bezalel speaks to our unconscious. This source confirms our artistic vocation that originated on Mount Sinai where the Tabernacle was birthed in the heart of God.

"The kind of work God usually calls you to is the kind of work (a) that you need most to do and (b) that the world most needs to have done."[2] This good rule is Frederick Buechner's further description of our vocation. As creative artists we naturally want to be involved in artistic ventures. This is what gladdens our heart and contributes to our well-being. There is fulfillment in the air when we are creating.

Suspended as we are between kairos and creos, we talk to the angels and sometimes we see God's face. It's hard to come down from Mount Sinai and face the ordinary dailiness of life. It's much easier to stay there and talk to God in rarefied air, Creator to created—BIG *C* to little *c*. How seductive it is to forget mundane necessities such as meals, family, sleep, social life, health, finances, job, and simply replace these unwelcome intrusions with creative output. We may secretly admit to ourselves that these needs are irrelevant, but our physical requirements and the outside world will come crashing in with their urgent needs in a most untimely manner and demand our immediate return to earth. So be it. Corita Kent quotes the Zen Master in *Learning by Heart:* "After ecstasy, the laundry."[3]

> *It's hard to come down from Mount Sinai and face the ordinary dailiness of life.*

37

When we have deep gladness about the work we most need to do, half of the good rule of vocation is complete. The other half requires discernment in community and in solitude, as there will be many different voices calling us to different kinds of work along life's journey. These voices may be legitimate and offer high rewards. But the source of the call is the question to discern. Who is calling us to our vocation? Is it the society, our culture, our ego, our mother, the church? Are we being called for a season—or for the duration?

All of these voices may point to good work that needs doing. But is it the voice of God . . . perhaps . . . speaking through the human voice or institution? Is the work to be done what most needs to be done in a field of critical needs? Will it animate our deep gladness, our gifts, our spiritual joy, our heavenly rapture? Can it draw us closer to Jesus? Will it develop partnership with God and others? Is there a sense of ecstasy—or is it mostly the laundry? Does it cause depression? Are we joyless, downcast in spirit? Fearful? Hoarding of our talent? Resentful? Bound to the clock? Living a fantasy life in our head?

The image of Christ will become known in those we serve as we live into God's calling.

In many cultures these questions will be asked in the context of the larger community, the tribe, the extended family, the ancestors. All of these questions are valid measures of discerning vocation and must be part of the holy equation. For some, the choice of vocation may be a once-in-a-lifetime decision; for others it will be a decision made again and again. Whatever the method we use, the decision is best ratified in the divine equation of partnership with God, the community of faith, and our own heart.

Bezalel must have surely learned more about his own skills as he worked on the Tabernacle. Nothing of its scope and nature had been constructed before, and Oholiab's assistance was a new model for leadership. Our calling will present many opportunities for growth. There will be joyful confirmation of our choice as well as wrenching questions about our calling. We may even doubt that we ever heard God's voice. As we seek to discern and fulfill our call in faith and integrity, using our creative gifts and abilities, we can be assured that our humanity will be more fully revealed, the meaning of our vocation made more clear. The image of Christ will become known in those we serve as we live into God's calling.

Partners in Creativity

Bezalel was called to his work and given a subcontractor, Oholiab, another skilled artist and teacher. The wisdom of God demonstrates that creativity is teachable and can be learned. Art has its own language and can be transmitted through its own peculiar alphabet and internal system.

When we are called to our vocation by God we are not left alone to figure it out by ourselves or work without resource. Like our creative ancestor Bezalel, we are given help and a community of people who need and want the gifts we have to offer. This may not be visible immediately, and we may have to search out resources, but they are there. Our creative gifts may even be employed to disclose where they are. The people of the Tabernacle brought a freewill offering of their everyday resources—jewelry, wood, cloth, stones, and other items—more than was needed until there was enough for the sanctuary: "for what they had already brought was more than enough to do all the work" (Exodus 36:7).

From the Exodus narrative we learn that Bezalel and Oholiab lived among scores of artistic Hebrews. The women also performed creative tasks and brought their crafts for the work. In Exodus 35:25-26, we learn that "all the skillful women spun with their hands, and brought what they had spun in blue and purple and crimson yarns and fine linen; all the women whose hearts moved them to use their skills spun the goats' hair." The women were involved in the ongoing work of the people.

The details of the Tabernacle call up a visual feast that dazzles the imagination. The daily activities of art, design, and structural integrity called upon the highest skill of each person as the tent of meeting took shape: the cutting and setting of precious stones, the holy garments for Aaron and Moses; the embellished columns and the carved wood, the twisted yarns and tassels, the gold inlay, the ark of the covenant, the columns, and the altars. The lavish beauty of each component creates an aesthetic picture of unrivaled heavenly glory, for beauty, worship, and practical use. In addition, the leadership model of Bezalel and Oholiab is an early example of mutual teamwork that is instructive for the church today as both leaders supervised workers and shared responsibilities.

The daily activities of art, design, and structural integrity called upon the highest skill of each person as the tent of meeting took shape.

40

In Praise of the Craft

To some, it may not be significant that art and particular kinds of creativity are described in the Bible. To those of us who want validation of our work, our vocation, and our love of artistic creation, however, the prominence of Bezalel is akin to God laying hands on our forehead with the blessing given to the stewards who used their talents wisely: "Well done, good and faithful servant! You have been faithful with a few things. I will put you in charge of many things. Come and share your master's happiness" (Matthew 25:21, NIV).

The Exodus chapters (and the subsequent description of the Jerusalem Temple, supervised by the craftsman, Huram-abi) show the esteem in which God holds these gifts and the importance of the people's participation in creating beauty that extols God's glory in nature, in the environment of worship, and in everyday living space. The artistry of Huram-abi is described in a letter to Solomon: "I have dispatched Huram-abi, a skilled artisan, endowed with understanding, the son of one of the Danite women, his father a Tyrian. He is trained to work in gold, silver, bronze, iron, stone, and wood, and in purple, blue, and crimson fabrics and fine linen, and to do all sorts of engraving and execute any design that may be assigned him, with your artisans, the artisans of my lord, your father David" (2 Chronicles 2:13-14).

The Tabernacle construction dissolves the false dichotomy between artistic design and crafting skill. Moses' description of Bezalel's qualifications was that God had "filled him with divine spirit, with ability, intelligence, and knowledge in every kind of craft"

41

(Exodus 31:3). Contemporary views impose a cultural hierarchy on artistic creation that sees craft making on the bottom rung of the so-called artistic ladder. Scripture proves it different. Skilled crafting requires a knowledge of the medium, be it words, paint, wood, or film, if the crafting artist is to determine its outcome.

In *State of the Arts*, Gene Veith, Jr., conveys the relation of craft to its maker: "The artist's dominion over matter involves intimacy and commitment, not tyranny or exploitation, as the object through infinite care and effort begins to conform to the artist's will."[4] History has shown that what is ultimately labeled art, or craft, may not have been the artist's intent at the outset. What begins as child's play, practical necessity, or sheer experimentation, is later viewed with high regard by history, critics, and public alike.

Simon Rodilla, builder of the unique Watts Towers in Los Angeles, combined experimentation and his intimacy with the land to construct his towering edifice solely of found objects, rubber tires, discarded plates, beer bottles, broken mirrors, and other signs of civilization's leftovers. When asked what inspired his vision, he said he wanted "to make something big on the landscape."[5] Today it inspires awe from visitors around the globe as a striking example of art from the heart of the people.

History has shown that what is ultimately labeled art, or craft, may not have been the artist's intent at the outset.

Likewise, our lives are enriched by the artistry of living quilts from centuries past that create a relationship to the women who stitched their constricted lives into small bits of cloth. At the same time, these hand-crafted quilts become objects of art

42

when separated from their practical use and displayed on gallery walls for aesthetic appreciation. The line between craft, decoration, function, and fine arts cannot be definitively drawn.

In the Tabernacle project, and dare we say in the eye of God, there is no distinction between high and low art. All the artistry is needed for the common good; the teaching of it, the making of it, the blessing of it. And all of it is infused with the Spirit of God. The Wisdom of Sirach (also known as Ecclesiasticus) elevates craft making to a necessity for the well-being of the community's social structure. "But they maintain the fabric of the world, / and their concern is for the exercise of their trade" (Sirach 38:34, Apocrypha).

What might we gain for the church today if we elevated a wider range of the arts to an activity that honors the worship of God and shapes our interaction with society? Who might we win for the cause of Christ if we proclaimed the arts as a vocation useful to the church and a pathway to spiritual discovery? The desire to make art and surround ourselves with beauty and art has a holy origin and impetus that originates in the early pages of our sacred history. Our inheritance from the chosen people of Israel comes with the imperative to continue the legacy of art for heaven's sake and earth's harmony. Bezalel not only gives us a biblical model and foundation for honoring the arts, but provides us a starting point for considering how the arts might be incorporated more broadly into the community of faith to honor our stewardship of God's holy vocation.

Who might we win for the cause of Christ if we proclaimed the arts as a vocation useful to the church and a pathway to spiritual discovery?

Reflections and Activities

1. How would you describe the work you are currently doing? Is it your vocation, your calling, interim work? Is it in the home? in the public arena?

2. List three experiences of deep gladness or spiritual joy associated with this work. Does this current work meet Buechner's category of "the world's deep hunger"?

3. What is needed to elevate creative expression and the arts to work that sustains the "fabric of the world"?

4. How would your church or faith community respond to a Potter's Guild, or Lawyer's Guild, or Writer's Guild as a bridge to discipleship and spiritual discovery? What might they have in common to deepen their faith and serve God through their vocation?

5. Design and propose a blessing ceremony, ritual, or vocational dedication for the creative artists in your group or congregation. Include verses from Bezalel's calling. Give each person a creative memento of the occasion.

6. Read Exodus 35–39 aloud with new eyes for seeing the panoramic view of the Tabernacle from inception to blessing. Keep a record of your reactions.

7. Give thanks to God for your calling with a creative offering to God—a poem, a song, a picture, collage, needlework; something you create yourself. Date it and put it in a special place.

CHAPTER 4

Don't Miss the Bliss

*B**liss:** great joy or happiness, spiritual joy, heavenly rapture, SYN. see ecstasy.*

If you've ever fallen in love you know the inexplicable state of bliss, the breathless euphoria and flutter that heightens every moment. The Bible's collection of love poems is a testament to the rapturous bliss of a man and wife. "There is a fragrance about you; / the sound of your name recalls it" (Song of Songs 1:3, TEV). Under the canopy of exuberant passion the lovers embrace the beauty of a woman in love: "Your lips cover me with kisses; / your love is better than wine" (1:2). The young man evokes images of his daily life in his description of his beloved's beauty: "Your hair dances like a flock of goats / bounding down the hills of Gilead. / Your teeth are as white as a flock of sheep / that have just been washed" (6:5-6). These lyrics of love invite us to feel the bliss, the passion, and the ecstasy God has already placed into the core of creation.

Bliss happens when we say yes to the creative stirring within us; yes to the sacred energy that calls us to our life's work and purpose. Bliss happens when the inner wisdom of our heart is confirmed in the community where we are known, trusted, and have a place. Bliss happens when our soul resonates with the world's needs and the desires of our heart find a home in shaping the future.

45

Creative Joy

"The artist," writes Rollo May in *The Courage to Create*, "at the moment of creating, does not experience gratification or satisfaction (though this may be the case later...). Rather, it is *joy*, joy defined as the emotion that goes with heightened consciousness, the mood that accompanies the experience of actualizing one's own potentialities."[1] At the completion of the Creation story we are given a glimpse of divine joy through a brief description of the Creator's fulfillment: "God saw everything that he had made, and indeed, it was very good" (Genesis 1:31).

The artist within each of us knows the inner peace and immense joy that exceeds mere words when a creative work has reached fruition. It is very good. These feelings of deep joy and accomplishment are more than self-congratulatory pats on the back. Bliss is the necessary antidote to lingering doubts that our creative doings and being are of permanent significance to God. The euphoria of the creative process is not an escape into our own self-centered world.

Our gifts were given for such a time as this and the Lord has need of them. The certainty of God's investment in us is spoken through the prophet Isaiah, confirming our most secret thoughts and desires. "Do not fear, for I have redeemed you; / I have called you by name, you are mine" (Isaiah 43:1). This affirmation is our deep gladness, our spiritual joy, our bliss.

Art students have been known to fall blissfully in love each time they paint a sunset. It's no wonder; the encounter with creativity awakens us to the world around us, filling us with awe and mystery over and over again. This same encounter is experienced by other artists: teachers, doctors, missionaries, home-makers, scientists, farm workers, and many, many, more. "Every person is a special kind of artist," says potter Mary Richards, "and every activity is a special art."[2] The truth of the universe is that creativity is not restricted to an elite group that society might call artists, but is available to each of us who is open to the creative encounter and to our own spirit.

Finding "That"

The artist lives within each of us. Every one of us is an imaginative person with an exceptional capacity to create beauty, to affect our life and the world around us. We may respond to the beauty of a sunset or a rose with a paintbrush or a camera, a song, or a little jig; whatever is expressive inside of us. The capacity to create and respond is not something we must learn; it is a divine gift and our birthright. But this natural ability suffers erosion as we modify our thinking and adjust our behavior to the prevailing thought of our day.

In our early years this truth of possessing natural gifts of creativity makes sense to us, but this inner knowing is diminished as we grow older and learn the world's realities. Kindergarten teachers know that they can ask their class, "How many of you can draw?" and every little hand will fly up in the air with excitement and confidence. On the other hand, a class of seventh graders will respond by pointing to one student, saying, "He's the artist in this class; he can draw." The notion that creativity is a natural part of being human is not taught or caught in such a way that we incorporate it into our self-image as we develop and grow. Whoever has learned to reproduce realistic images is the one we recognize as the artist among us.

Betty Edwards, innovative art teacher and author of *Drawing on the Right Side of the Brain,* speaks of learning how to trick the brain in order to draw. "From an early age, perhaps the age of eight or nine, I was able to draw fairly well. I think I was one of those few children who accidentally stumble upon a way of seeing that enables one to draw well. I can still remember saying to myself, even as a young child, that if I wanted to draw something, I had to do 'that.' I never defined 'that,' but I was aware of having to *gaze* at whatever I wanted to draw for a time until 'that' occurred. Then I could draw with a fairly high degree of skill for a child."[3]

Most of us have no concept of "that" and do not know how to catch on to it. The idea of shifting to brain modes appropriate for particular skills is not a common approach to learning in our Western educational system. So the creative side of our brain that learns by rich, visual images and associative patterns is left to progress on its own, by hit or miss. Many of us then, must be content with meager attempts at creativity that miss most of the bliss that encourages and fuels our growth forward. Our encounter with the diverse manifestations of creativity around us is likewise stunted as we are not able to make the connections to our own capacity for self-expression.

So the creative side of our brain that learns by rich, visual images and associative patterns is left to progress on its own, by hit or miss.

Creative Ecstasy

Many creative people describe the experience of spiritual oneness and connecting to the universe that comes from their creative activity. But the vast majority of us remain spectators to this enlivening connection; it seems to elude our ability to touch or receive. Our interaction with God's creative Spirit cannot be determined by a paintbrush, a scroll saw, a lump of clay, or a set of vocal cords. We must permit ourselves to respond with whatever is inside of us. Traditional definitions and ingrained cultural standards must give way if we are to break free and discover our bliss, our authentic ecstasy, our *ex-statis*, our being drawn out of ourselves, the "outgoingness" that ignites and fuels our participation in the giftedness of our world.

Rollo May tells us in *The Courage to Create*[4] that the paradox of ecstasy is that when we stand out from ourselves, letting go of the various parts or fragments of ourselves, we become all of ourselves, more than our separated selves, and united into one whole. Creative ecstasy is not limited to the individual experience but can be a corporate phenomenon that is generated when a deep spiritual connection happens within a group that embraces creative work together.

Such was the case at the beginning of this millennium when the world-acclaimed artist-in-wood, Sam Maloof, dedicated his hand-carved altar furniture commissioned by a seminary, to the memory and honor of Freda, his wife of fifty-three years. During the service of dedication, participants offered numerous tributes, read Scripture, and expressed gratitude to God for her creative life and artistic support of her husband. "Some Enchanted Evening," her favorite song, was sung during the afternoon. Each note from the soloist gently fell like a petal from a rose as we, the audience, were enclosed in a gift of unexpected bliss. The hush that followed was a silent witness to our heightened connection to the family and one another.

Through the spoken words of meditation and remembrances, we, who were a diverse collection of family, friends, and guests, were united in a chorus of praise and thanksgiving for God's gift of mutual devotion and artistry in the Maloof family. As guests mingled in the chancel area, touching the twenty-foot cross and rubbing hands along the fluted edge of the natural-grained table altar and stately candleholders, there was a deep bond between object and subject. We were one with the art, one with the artist and marriage companion whom we honored. God's ecstasy enabled us to transcend our limited vision of creative art within the human family and embrace a greater vision of family as a repository of God's gifts—perhaps a glimpse of the new age of God already breaking in on us.

Creativity as a Bridge to God

In every culture and wisdom tradition, creativity connects us to the Spirit and invites us to be more than we thought we could be. As Jeremy Begbie puts it in *Voicing Creation's Praise,* "Art we choose to call inspired will inevitably possess something of an eschatological quality.... Art which truly bears the imprint of the Spirit will thus not so much hark back to an imagined paradise, as anticipate within space and time, provisionally but substantially, the final transfiguration of the cosmos."[5] The awe-filled encounter of the afternoon with creative artistry confirmed again how the marriage of beauty and function in the service of God makes visible that which had not been seen before. Art is love made visible.

Ecstasy is an intensity of consciousness that occurs in the creative act, uniting form and passion with order and vitality. This dimension of creativity invites us to bring our whole selves to the creative enterprise—our reason and our passion, our rationality and our emotion. We find this view of creativity expressed in Rollo May's *The Courage to Create:* "It involves the total person, with the subconscious and the unconscious acting in unity with the conscious. It is not, thus, irrational, it is rather, suprarational. It brings intellectual, volitional, and emotional functions into play all together."[6]

We may think our creativity dwarfs in comparison to the high art that sets the standards around us and labels our endeavors as merely hobbies, paint-by-the-numbers, or weekend leisure. To the contrary, whether we are carving wood into a cross, writing a poem, making children's lunches, or reading for the blind, we are having God-talk in the language of the heart, a vocabulary fashioned by God and intimately known before we speak it. Our creative gifts are a bridge to God and the world unlike any other and should not be dismissed as trivial or unworthy.

Whether we are carving wood into a cross, writing a poem, making children's lunches, or reading for the blind, we are having God-talk.

It is our courageous step of bringing something new into being whose end we do not know but are willing to trust. Do we feel uncertain in elevating our creative gifts to the level that encounters the world or dialogues with the divine? Yes, we do. Have we been encouraged to do this through the church's teaching, or other means? No, we have not. Remember that until recently our creative gifts and pursuits were thought to be outside of our spiritual life and outside of the study, concern, or serious development by the church, except as it fit into its ongoing mission.

Finding God Through Our Creativity

This attitude is beginning to change. We are finding that creative expression is a meaningful and vocational activity for many persons in the church who benefit from bringing their part-time and full-time pursuits and creative professions under the transforming gospel of Christ. The words of the psalmist capture this panoramic view of life that acknowledges the God of our entire personhood: "O LORD, you have searched me and known me. / You know when I sit down and when I rise up; / you discern my thoughts from far away.... / Even before a word is on my tongue, / O LORD, you know it completely.... / Such knowledge is too wonderful for me; / it is so high that I cannot attain it" (Psalm 139:1-2, 4, 6).

The glory of God is beyond our definition and moves in and through our universe and our lives in ways we cannot engineer or fathom. As we are faithful to the gifts that reside within us, giving them expression to be used in this world, we give courage to others to recognize their gifts. For many people this is the path by which they will come to know a deeper reality of the spirit of Christ—through the gifts of creativity they see and feel and express themselves. Our task is to be faithful to the gifts we have been given for the greater glory of God.

Being More Than Ourselves

When we are creating, we are in kairos/creos time, neither young nor old, neither past nor future. We are in eternal time, an "altered" state, not bound by time or space, so that we converse with cave painters who drew symbols on rocks and cave walls, and we hear the voices of creativity yet to be born. The artist within us must look both ways if we would speak to our own age and to future generations.

This dynamic interaction of the past and future is not simply a product of artistic subjectivity but the quality of art itself to disclose life and truth beyond and before itself. During times of high creativity many persons say they are aware of a presence, an energy at work within them that is greater than they are. There is an awareness of the unseen hand in their work, a recognition that what is coming from them is more than they could offer by themselves.

We in the faith community put a sacred name to it: God, Holy Spirit, divine presence, angels, spirit of Christ. Whatever name we give it, an altered state, universal consciousness, we know that there is something within us that is beyond us that cannot be ignored.

When we are open to God's Spirit our creative gifts are used to touch each other's lives and show the face of Christ. An urgent need in my nephew's life came to me through a language I know well—music. One morning upon waking I "saw" musical notes that were left over from dream time; they hung from invisible threads in the air and appeared as fresh laundry pinned to a clothesline. I read the notes just as if they were placed on a music staff, following the melody over and over again, especially the peak in the first phrase so I wouldn't forget it.

Standing at the piano I found some manuscript paper and jotted down each note just as it appeared in my head. The more I wrote, the more notes there were to be written. After a while there were words: "Feel the love, it's all around your way. It's the promise of a new, a bright tomorrow. Feel the love, it's with you every day. It's a light to keep you safe along the way."

Even before I received the words, I knew the notes contained deep supporting love as they blew with the wind like clothes on a laundry line in spring. After the first round of scribbles I sensed the dream song was more than a pretty tune. It was an assignment. I called my mid-twenties nephew and invited him over to talk about his life. The dream song moved me to prayer and action—and prayer again.

The persistent love of God speaks to us in the language of our heart—in dreams, music, clay, canvass, the wind, the mountains; through color and stones; and we learn again that creativity is a collaborative process between the Spirit, our gift, and our yes. Our part of the process is to watch and pray—to listen and be attentive to that divine presence, the voice of the holy, the flap of angel wings and notes in the breeze. Then we act.

Plumbing the Depths

Creativity involves plumbing the depths; it's more than making things, although we may make them later. Creative yearnings urge us to dig deep enough to touch the mystery that inhabits all things—in the earth and above the earth. The gift we have to give to the universe is already known in the heart of God, who keeps whispering it to us. When this ability is acknowledged in our heart and coached into birth, our spirit is at one with the Creator and at rest in ourselves. We then know the deepest part of us has been heard and blessed into being.

There is a spirit song that vibrates within us—a song we can sing without words—it is the song of the soul, the something within us that connects us to our source. When we allow ourselves to be a channel for that source of divine love and inspiration, God creates through us and the work is not hard. We are open to wider worlds, and we hear songs waiting to be sung, dances asking to be choreographed, pots wanting to be shaped, patterns asking to be quilted through willing hands that are open and receptive. Then the work of creating is not a labor. It flows through us and the words of Jesus resonate through our gifts: "My yoke is easy, and my burden is light" (Matthew 11:30).

Like Mary, the mother of Jesus, we become the obedient servant of the work. It comes to us asking to be born, to be given shape and voice through our gift, like an annunciation. And if we would be at peace with ourselves, our reply must be that of Mary, "Let it be with me according to your word" (Luke 1:38). The urgent need in my nephew's life came knocking through a dream song I couldn't ignore, in a language I know fluently. Peace came when I sang the song and obeyed its call.

When we allow ourselves to be a channel for divine love and inspiration, God creates through us and the work is not hard.

55

From the Heart of God

A pink camellia tree just outside my patio door is home to several hummingbirds that visit the large blossoms from October to March. One year I hung one of those plastic bird feeders with red homemade nectar from a roof overhang. The feeder box said that the wings of a hummingbird flap over seventy-five times a second. As one of these small birds darted past me on its way to the feeder, I heard the deep flutter of its fragile wings, and I wondered what angel wings sound like, winnowing the air. The supreme artistry of God reminds us in the tiniest of creatures that we are cared for in our needs too.

Our abilities are a reflection of God's grace—nothing that we can take much credit for. We show our love for the giver when we use the gifts over and over. The love of the Creator that connects us to all of nature's creatures gives us appreciation for God's gift giving that we in our small way try to imitate.

The voice of God speaks to that something within us that goes beyond the creativity of the marketplace. Our gift may be the primary place where a need can be met and a service can be rendered for heaven's sake. The mystery of faith is that it spills outside our neatly arranged frame of reference and arrests our dozing senses with love songs at dedications, nature in winter, and dreams clipped to a spring clothesline. We hold these treasures in earthen vessels surrounded by the flutter of angel wings. Bliss.

Reflections and Activities

1. Creativity begins with a listening heart just as Mary listened to the angel. How would you answer these questions: What wants to be said through me? What wants to be done through me? What wants to be given through me?

2. Have you answered as Mary or tried another way? What was the result?

3 Your body can help you recognize your gifts. When have you felt you were standing in the presence of the holy? What were the signs? Have sweaty or cold hands, butterflies in your stomach, or dry mouth, ever been indications that you were in the presence of something special, or your gifts were in use or needed?

4. In what ways has God "spoken" to you? Is there a language or activity through which you feel close to God? Share the outcome.

5. Sometimes we are inspired to dig deeper into the wellspring of our own creativity. It can be as simple as trying a tool or a recipe we've never used before. List three ways you have begun to dig deeper into your creative gifts.

6. Describe creative bliss. What needs to happen for you to experience it?

CHAPTER 5

Trusting Our Creative Spirit

*A*bandoning our creativity is detrimental to our health. Our spiritual well-being takes a dive when we close ourselves off from this natural expression of God's gifts within us. Our physical and emotional health suffers as well. Internal equilibrium is thrown off balance by the loss of our creative center, and we wake up to a spiritual malaise, unable to tap into the joy of our faith or the vitality of our creative gifts, the external expression of our belief in Christ.

Our oldest and wisest self knows the voice of our creativity that must be heeded if we are to be whole and healthy. Stewart Brand, editor of the *Whole Earth Catalogue,* says: "The voices that you need to hear, whisper, slowly and infrequently. The only way to hear them is listen.... There's a difference between intention driving us on, and mystery pulling us on. Mystery will always educate and correct. Intention can go off the end of its own limb."[1]

Filling the Void

Minnietta Millard felt an emptiness growing in her soul after graduating from Boston University School of Theology with a degree in Christian Education.

"After eight years in the church I knew I was not using my creativity as I should. I felt dry. It was very hard because my husband was the pastor and he had looked forward to our being in ministry together . . . for ever and ever. We both had. This is what I studied and worked for during three long years of graduate courses. I decided to take the battery of tests at a Career Counseling Center. This confirmed the void in my soul that yearned to be filled by art.

"I continued my position in the church as I discerned God's voice and direction for my life. Towards the end of that period of seeking I saw an article in our local newspaper about a woman who made glass boxes. I had never thought about this kind of art before, but my heart leaped inside me as I read, and suddenly I 'knew,' I just knew, that glass was the medium for me.

"I had never cut a piece of glass in my life so I found a beginning class in leaded glass making. During that Sunday evening class I was sure it was God's voice that had led me to this place. The following Tuesday I resigned my position at the church. It was the right thing to do. The handling of the glass and the tools seemed made for my hands. It was my personal epiphany that shone through the shards of colored glass—my calling had found me.

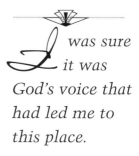

I was sure it was God's voice that had led me to this place.

"Twenty-two years after I saw the hand of God reflected in a sheet of translucent glass, my husband and I are still in ministry together. My altar can be found in the Sunshine Reflections Studios, the business I started where I fabricate glass installations, including a 15 x 18 foot stained glass panel installed in the church where my husband and I share a special ministry together."[2] Minnietta listened to her heart and found her way back home...and back to the world.

It takes courage to stay awake in the middle of the night to hear what God's Spirit is saying to us. It's much easier to turn over and go back to sleep, flip on the voice of the radio, plan a meeting agenda, read a book, or just eat another piece of gooey cherry pie. It is a scary thing to turn in a direction that is different from our preparation, from what other people expect of us, demand from us, or have paid and prayed for us to do. Creativity takes courage; whether it feels like a BIG *C* or a little *c*, courage is required to be true to our inmost self.

A Different Way of Knowing

The temptation to resist this kind of transcendent knowing can be as great as the call to heed it. We swing back and forth like a broken pendulum on a grandfather clock that is wound too tight, swaying from side to side, out of sync with the appointed hour. Often our first reaction to the Spirit's tug is to turn away and deny what we are feeling, labeling it nonsense, crazy, selfish—our own fear of flying. But this experience of direct knowing is shared by the famous, the infamous, the near and never famous. It is a knowledge that comes from beyond our self, a kind of relentless announcement that something wants to be told and be known, be seen and be sung, be spoken, be danced, be made and be loved through us.

In the marrow of our bones we know that this something must be accomplished—a task, a discovery, an image, a design, a beginning, an ending, a releasing, a holding, a healing; and it has an appointed time among the galaxies. It is shrouded in mystery, yet we know it is real. This repeated call is our annunciation, the proclamation to us, from within us, that God has readied the *kairos* to embrace the constellation of our creative abilities for this particular moment.

This knowledge, spoken of by Karl Rahner in *Spirit in the World,*[3] is "pre-concept," a kind of "preapprehension" or knowledge that is beyond the horizon of our knowing, yet that which is knowable but not yet known, which is an infinite progression. When this intense "pre"-knowing comes, it cannot be ignored. It is accompanied by a certainty that will not be denied and from which we cannot hide. To do so would be at the peril of our soul.

Even though we do not know where this voice might take us if we follow, it resonates with something deep in our spirit that answers back with a recognition and yearning that leaps over our cognitive faculties. What we are hearing is the premonition of our birth—and death—and birth again as something tells us that this is more than a temporary change. It is the beginning of a transformation, a prelude to transcendence that will require a death of some kind if we are going to give birth to the fullness of our creative gifts. There is an imminence to this knowing; it must begin now, even if we wait until the morning.

A Voice in the Night

My mother tells me (I vaguely remember this) that when I was nine years old, I was awakened in the night three times with a message for her from God. Each time I woke up I fell out of bed but did not obey the voice I heard telling me to give her the message. Instead, I picked myself off the floor and climbed back into my bed. It must be true that the third time's a charm because the third nudge from God sent me down the hallway to her bedroom where I shook my mother awake and tearfully delivered the message: *"G—G—God . . . s—s—said . . . y—you . . . sh—sh—should . . . p—p—p—pray . . . m—m—more."* After her initial shock and disbelief, Mom comforted me with soothing hugs and reassured me that it was OK to speak to her in this authoritative way. I returned to my bed and slept peacefully without interruption until morning.

In recent years I've learned that my mother was indeed struggling with the decision of whether to change from the church and denomination where our family had given many years of service and leadership. The reluctant obedience of a nine-year-old showed her the way to discern God's voice in her ambivalence. That was the year our family entered The Methodist Church, a move prompted and led by the Spirit. It was a hard decision but one we could follow as we were led by the Spirit of God.

Heeding the voice that continues to prod can lead to a place of greater fulfillment and service to God in the larger domain.

Not all our choices are as dramatic as this, but heeding the voice that continues to prod can lead to a place of greater fulfillment and service to God in the larger domain. Whether it happens in quantum leaps or incremental steps, courageous trust is required to discern and dialogue, to act and keep on acting in the light of God's revelation, which may be very different from our best-laid plans and other perceptions of our gifts and our life.

My mother surely did not expect

that her nine-year-old daughter would point the way to the family's future. Nine-year-olds are not programmed to concern themselves with such weighty matters as denominational changes. But God chose to be known through an unsuspecting child who bore a divine message of exhortation to pray. A degreed director of religious education did not expect to discover the path to the vocation of her heart in a newspaper article. But she did. The nature of this God who speaks through a child and appears in the media is often incognito among us, as revealed in the incredulous question of Matthew 25:37, "Lord, when was it that we saw you...?"

God of the Right Brain

Urban Holmes, Episcopal priest, seminary professor, and author of *Ministry and Imagination*, describes this God of our peripheral vision: "God appears somewhere over my left shoulder."[4] This supreme artist God hovers at the edge of our consciousness, operating beyond our control and intimately known in contexts of nonrational visions and impossible dreams.

The experience of direct knowing, direct connection, and mystical experience of creative flow, leans first on the God of the "right brain," the left shoulder, the awakened mind. Artists of every description know the flow or the "white light" of the right brain and have used every tool imaginable to affect this shift to the "side" of the brain that initiates high creative output.

The synergistic interaction of our spirit and our brain continues to intrigue brain scientists and researchers of human powers. Although the complexity of the brain defies simple separation into right and left halves, this visual image of the dual brain is helpful in our assessment of current educational methods, our preferred way to view the world, and the processes we are most comfortable with. What we call the "right brain" experience is the modality associated with direct knowing. It gives us access to a different reality or a consciousness that bypasses the rational mind, reasonable doctrine, and ordered analysis. If we give it permission, this mode of knowing is hospitable to altered states of consciousness such as hypnosis, meditation, remote viewing, ecstatic experiences, and athletic "psych-up."

A primary key to achieving this altered state or nonordinary reality where we find the God of spontaneous prayers and nonwritten liturgy is our willingness to surrender, to let go of control over outcomes, to see things differently, to value risk, and to live willingly with ambiguity. This arena, if pursued, has the greatest potential to show us the missing parts of ourselves, the self that Jesus said will do more than he did; the hidden self that knows God intimately and wholly, without reserve. This knowing is akin to the mountaintop experience of conversion, filling with the Holy Spirit, baptism, healing, gift of tongues, spiritual visions, forgiveness, reconciliation, and other ecstatic experiences of the spirit.

We feel the presence of the early church and the Spirit power Jesus promised at his ascension.

When we make these connections to direct knowing in the setting of the church and faith community, what joy we feel in the corporate consciousness that shares spiritual unity and power. We feel the presence of the early church and the Spirit power Jesus promised at his ascension. This unity enables us to give birth to the creative artist within us, to recover our unique gifts, and to release them for the glory of God, our own spiritual fulfillment, and the blessing of the earth.

Many people in our churches are consciously seeking this kind of knowing and come away sad when it is not offered or found year after year in their church community. Fear among the uninitiated and horror stories of leaders who approached it without preparation or sensitivity prevent us from pursuing this birthright of direct knowing that is rooted in spiritual history and biblical tradition.

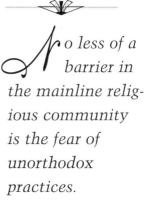

No less of a barrier in the mainline religious community is the fear of unorthodox practices.

L. Robert Keck, United Church of Christ minister, writes of this deep desire for precognitive knowing in *The Spirit of Synergy,* his insightful book that grew out of his long-term physical pain and a search for healing. Our cultural dismissal of power in this arena of altered consciousness is described by Keck as fear. "We have by and large been unfamiliar with them, feared them, refused to consider them 'scientific,' and assigned labels to them like 'occult' that allow us to dismiss them. Yet it is increasingly clear that altered states of consciousness are the key to releasing vast portions of our untapped abilities and are certainly involved in a full life of meaning and purpose."[5]

No less of a barrier in the mainline religious community is the fear of unorthodox practices, lack of legitimacy in seminary training, and the weight of tradition. Keck includes the church as an institution that chooses not to tap the vast human resource in this area: "Contemporary Christianity, education, and medical care, for instance, almost totally ignore the potential in altered states of consciousness. They have consequently been missing vast areas of rich resources by which a person can find meaning spiritually, gain and use knowledge, and play an active role in creating and maintaining health."[6]

Whether we are searching for the vocation that nurtures our spirit or wrestling with life's thorny issues, using the full range of our abilities can bring us surprising enlightenment when we know how to tap into our deep creative wells in partnership with our intuitive processes. Whatever means we use to enter the creative flow, be it prayer, dance, music, or a Tai-Bo video, the goal is to de-activate the mind that plans grocery lists and grades papers and activate the mind that welcomes creative interplay. Without this different consciousness we are numb to the best of our creative thoughts.

States of Consciousness

Betty Edwards, artist, teacher, and author, helps us connect to Holmes's image of a "left-sided" God and the "right-sided brain" with a chart used in her drawing classes. According to R-Mode and L-Mode characteristics, shorthand terms coined by Edwards, the locus of direct knowing, deep discernment, high creativity, and communion with the Spirit are found in the right brain modality. These definitions are not fixed categories, as the complexity of the brain cannot be reduced to two distinct halves; but they help us understand our unique approach to life, and different kinds of mental processing.

Characteristics of L-Mode and R-Mode [7]

L-Mode	**R**-Mode
VERBAL: Using words to name, describe, define.	NONVERBAL: Visual, perceptual awareness of things, with minimal connection with words.
ANALYTIC: Figuring things out step-by-step or part-by-part.	SYNTHETIC: Putting things together to form wholes.
SYMBOLIC: Using a symbol to *stand for* something. For example, the drawn form ☜ stands for eye, the sign + stands for the process of addition.	REAL: Relating to actual things as they are, at the present moment, in all their concrete, perceptual complexity.
CATEGORICAL: Naming general groups of concepts.	METAPHORICAL: Seeing likenesses between things; understanding metaphorical relationships and analogies.
TEMPORAL: Keeping track of time. Sequencing one thing after another— doing first things first, second things second, etc.	NONTEMPORAL: Without a sense of linear time.
RATIONAL: Drawing conclusions based on *reason* and *facts*.	NONRATIONAL: Not requiring a basis of reason or facts: willingness to suspend judgment and risk guessing based on "seeing things differently."

DIGITAL: Using numbers as in counting.

SPATIAL: Seeing where things are in relation to other things, and how parts go together to form a whole.

LOGICAL: Drawing conclusions based on logic: one thing following another in logical order, for example, a mathematical theorem or a well-stated argument.

INTUITIVE: Making leaps of insight, often based on incomplete patterns, hunches, feelings, or visual images.

LINEAR: Thinking in terms of linked ideas, one following another, leading to a convergent conclusion.

GLOBAL: Seeing whole things all at once; perceiving the many facets of a problem or situation simultaneously, often leading to divergent, multiple conclusions.

Clues to a Different World

Direct knowing is not the same as knowledge in the intellectual sense. It is qualitatively different from being "knowledgeable" or thinking analytically. Nor should it be confused with accumulating information in the L-Mode way. Direct or inner knowing comes from a different source, although it can be tripped off by traditional learning methods; books, lectures, study, classes, research, reason, and facts.

Just as none of us uses one kind of mental process to the exclusion of another, direct knowing relies on intuition, imagination, paradox, and ambiguity, but not exclusively. There may be conversations with L-Mode but usually at a later time after the perceptual methods are used first. Because we are acculturated in rational, analytical processes, it is important to delay going directly to them until we have immersed ourselves in the intuitive way of knowing.

Direct knowing relies on intuition, imagination, paradox, and ambiguity, but not exclusively.

Other brain research that is helping to interpret the brain's activities is the use of the electroencephalograph (EEG) to "measure" states of conscienousness. This machine measures the electrical impulses coming off the surface of the brain, and these impulses, called brain waves, are recorded on a paper readout. Although brain-wave research is in its infancy, we do know that certain waves are higher and faster than others and are present during certain experiences, from the deep sleep of the DELTA waves to the emergency reactions, high creativity, and ecstatic consciousnesss of HIGH BETA frequencies. Our culture and our church have a preference for the beta consciousness equated with ordinary waking activities and intellectual and verbal activity.

In my own work as a jeweler and gourd artist, direct knowing can be translated as direct collaboration with the Holy Spirit. While "fiddling around" one morning with some leftover gourd pieces in my "studio" (studio = wet bar converted to working space where everything I need is visible on wall shelves and within reach), I pondered my wearable art designs from an earlier period that were guided by intuition and a strong connection to ancestral art and cave drawings. I remembered the sensation of ancient presence as I combined various found objects: stones, feathers, metal, bone, gourd, and dyes.

69

On this morning, I discovered that the more I fiddled at various combinations, the more each piece came together in an unstructured, imaginative way, as if guided by unseen hands from another time. I decided to go with the flow. After a few minutes the "I" that makes decisions was no longer needed except as a conduit to pick up pieces and lay them down in combinations that I seemed to already know. A kind of creative frenzy took over as I abandoned myself to the unity of the artistic movement. Even my VOJ (voice of judgment) took a walk so my creative explorer was free to play and explore without censure. It seemed that all the while I was working I also stood aside, watching what was unfolding, like a kind of lucid dream where you know you're dreaming even while the action takes place.

After a while the feeling of compulsion subsided and I sat down with a sigh . . . slightly out of breath. It was over. Later I surveyed what "we" had created and wondered "who *really* made that?" The public response to work made during these early morning sessions of intuitive abandon fueled by the presence of ancient allies confirms the circle of direct knowing. Those who see these pieces also become connected beyond time and space to the creative powers that hear the voices that want to speak through us.

My VOJ (voice of judgment) took a walk so my creative explorer was free to play and explore without censure.

From one appreciative buyer: "I suppose you are aware that your creations manifest themselves as goddesses. I don't know what's in your mind when these fire, earth, and water elements come together in your hands; but they seem to be beings in their own right."

70

Direct knowing can be equated with the illumination phase of the creative process. Sometimes it comes in a flash of certainty, other times it is slow in coming; meandering into our consciousness, picking its way through our definitions and conclusions to show us a different route to our goal. In spite of its circuitous route we can aid the process by being attentive, by keeping our mental antennae up and waving. The clues that help us tap into our inner knowledge are nearby if we choose to follow them. Discovery is often at the end of the long road that begins with the nonverbal R-Mode, whose methods may appear to be a waste of time, "touchy—feely" nonsense, or manufacturing our own reality.

Fear of ridicule and embarrassment have hampered our growth and fulfillment.

Healing and intercessory prayer are steeped in these R-Mode methods that require a suspension of sequential, linear logic. Stories abound about knowledge that comes to us in nonrational ways that proves to be useful and effective. But we are often reluctant to accept it or act on it for fear of ridicule and lack of verification.

Prerequisites for growing along this direct route to the Spirit of God are basic: a safe place to explore the realm of the Spirit, trusted leadership, biblical support, a caring community, and the assurance that we are not crazy. Fear of ridicule and embarrassment, fear of being a beginner in this area of Christian experience have hampered our growth and fulfillment from the benefits of direct knowing. The giggle factor is a dominant inhibitor of our access to God's Spirit in the world and in us. And yet, this persistent tugging will not go away. We may be closer than we realize to direct or transcendent knowing.

Staying Awake to the Signs

A clue to our proximity is a persistent, agitated, or wandering mind. "She doesn't seem to be with us" is a common observation of someone seeking to know God in this way. Often mislabeled as mental laziness or lack of concentration, it can awaken us to the tugging at our creative spirit to come along and follow where it leads. Like a child who will not stop pulling on her mother's sleeve until she gets the attention she demands, in public or private, this plea to be noticed is persistent, even when her mother is embarrassed or occupied.

The call for recognition does not observe social etiquette or customary rules for L-Mode learning. It is often interruptive, raising disturbing questions about accepted truth, and upsetting the predictable sequence of cause and effect where one thing follows another: A + B = C. Direct knowing can erupt in an explosion of simultaneous hypotheses and conclusions, or the presentation of the one exquisitely right answer.

In traditional learning we are chided for staring into space, exhibiting a glassy-eyed look, dozing, or following the flight of a bird outside a church sanctuary window. The L-Mode method demands that we pay strict attention, stay awake, be alert, sit up straight. These implicit rules for learning are communicated to young and old alike. But when we direct our alertness to the voice that calls to us from the the inner flight of our imagination, we discover more of the pathway that leads to knowing of a different kind.

How often have we found our attention interrupted by a word or phrase and missed part of a lecture, or sermon, or presentation? We were startled to realize that our inner mind had traveled to a deeper place. When we "came back to our self," we discovered that the story line or sermon or prayer had shifted, even ended without our knowing it, though our body was present the whole time. The power of creative expression (a movie, a dance, a drama, a garden, a meditation, a tennis tournament) can invite us through the door that leads to another reality, revealing precious knowledge of the soul—ours and that of the community.

Physical signs in our bodies alert us to our direct knowing. Sweaty palms, a butterfly stomach, tears, sleepiness, dry mouth, ringing ears, pain, a burning in our stomach are not just signs of panic or anxiety or indigestion; they can be an apprehension of the Spirit's movement around us if we are willing to test it. There is also a heightened sense of creativity and empowerment during these times, when we find our vital energy is charged, ready to be put to use. These physical signs can also be clues to the anointing of the Spirit for a special task.

External confirmation is yet another sign that tells us a different knowledge resides within us. "You always seem to know what is happening when others can't see it," we are told, or "You have just what we need to plan a program, to lead a retreat. Come be our leader." Others notice our comfort and capacity in this realm of direct knowing and ask, "How did you know that?" Or maybe, "I wish you would speak out more about these kinds of things. We need to hear more from you, or your prayers always hit the target." This connection to the Spirit is

Physical signs in our bodies alert us to . . . an apprehension of the Spirit's movement around us.

73

made more noticeable when it is used in settings where it is not usually practiced or has grown cold.

External confirmation also comes through career testing, talking through our plans with spiritual directors, professional counselors, prayer partners, and trusted friends. Most often it is the inner voice of the R-Mode that values incubation, nuance, visual image, and metaphor, that is less audible and likely to be shoved aside for the L-Mode categories of logical thought and step-by-step progression.

The outer voices that speak with more volume, more logical reasoning, and more often, can overpower the inner voice that pleads for attention and a fair hearing. This is the time to give your linear brain some homework. Ask it to monitor your breathing, send it off to survey your environment. Soon it will settle down and take a nap while you attend to the mental process that reads by pictures and perceptions.

Discernment—Digging Deeper

Discernment is the biblical word closest to direct knowing that brings insight and meaning to events and activities not immediately revealed through other ways. Too often when discernment is a group activity it omits the R-mode methods that dig deeper than analysis and research alone. This shared ability to know beyond the concrete is a corporate way of seeing in the dark that looks to many persons for direction. The landscape of the spirit is too large, too complex, to be approached with one modality, or partial brain learning. We must bring the whole brain and the whole body to the whole spirit.

Direct knowing and spiritual discernment are not

the private property of an elite few. Rather they are available to any who would open themselves to the wider journey of the spirit and trust God's providence. We marvel at the ability of some people to access this gift; but these are human abilities already implanted within us, like the desire to laugh or cry.

It's intriguing to ponder what we might discover if we more readily shared the intuitive knowledge that comes to us. We might adapt the habit of the aboriginal people of Australia and bring the mystery of our night dreams to the daylight and plumb their depth for fresh insight inside the family setting. We can only imagine the insight and discernment our children might develop if we gave them the tools at an early age to plumb the depths of their dreams for meaning, direction, and self-knowledge. We might go beyond the family grouping of the breakfast table and explore our dreams at the business planning table. We might bring the steps for insight into dreams to a staff meeting to help one another discern the clues from God that are embedded in dream symbols.

Direct knowing and spiritual discernment are not the private property of an elite few.

Our intuitive leaps would be the subject of group discussions. Cross-cultural and inter-religious ways of discerning the Spirit would be as commonly recognized as other spiritual practices. What might emerge from our work-related settings if we met once a week to share recent dreams or visionary nudges about work relationships, job fulfillment, and product quality and innovation? Imagine a staff meeting where we focus on the gifts and creative capacities of our colleagues in order to support and call them forth and nurture them. Could not the church benefit from

75

embracing the over fifty dreams and visions in the Old and New Testaments as valid ways to vision our ministries forward?

In many ways the artist is the visionary or shaman among us—exposing inner vulnerability, willing to sustain the trance and anointing of the Spirit to take flights into undiscovered worlds and return with creative knowledge and healing symbols that benefit the whole community. The new work of the larger body becomes transformational as they tutor others in their power to access these capacities in themselves.

By seeing the world through these nontraditional openings, we gain access to another part of our being and the mystery of God's Spirit. We are more than we know we are, possessing a knowledge that drinks from a deep well of God's Spirit and shares in God's greater knowledge. This knowing prompts us to act in direct ways commensurate with our knowing. So we read to preschool children once a week; we join a work team to Bolivia; we become a new style missionary that advocates for runaway teens; we adopt a child, enter therapy, speak the truth; we sever toxic ties; we go to church; we join a picket line and recommit to justice. Not only do we see differently, we know differently; we act differently for the sake of a different future. And we finally yield to the gift that has pursued us, knocking at the door of our heart, wanting to be heard and invited into our lives. Jesus promised many rooms in the house of God. Our trust of God's Spirit leads us to the rooms in God's house where our gifts are expanded to bring the universe closer to the divine vision for eternity.

In many ways the artist is the visionary or shaman among us.

A Different Kind of Teacher

Learning to hear the voices that prod us to befriend our creative spirit moves us closer to communion with our own soul. With the help of trusted teachers, we can walk backward through our lives and trace the tilts and turns that responded to a deeper knowing. We are not starting from zero. These shifts are still inside us.

During the times that we do need a spiritual director to help us, a friend of God, a counselor, a prayer partner, a guide, a muse, it is important to know someone skilled at navigating the road of the soul and reading the signs along the way. We need someone who can remind us that our bodies hold stored memories of direct, life-giving experience that can show us the way through rough times and crucial decisions when this memory has been recovered. Like a medical doctor, these are relationships that we should cultivate before a crisis of the spirit is upon us.

The capacity to tap into this knowledge that is buried, forgotten, or repressed, is within our reach; we just don't know how or where to reach so we can activate this dormant ability. The creative tools that open this treasure of hidden knowledge of the soul are not taught in the same way we teach plane geometry, English grammar, or football charts; yet they are just as accessible.

In *Drawing on the Artist Within, Dr.* Betty Edwards points out the fallacy of our attitude toward drawing that is not applied to the teaching of reading. "Just be free!" "Use your imagination!" "Reading should be fun!" Teachers would simply "supply lots of reading materials for children to handle and manipulate and then wait to see what happens." Who would read with such a casual approach to instruction?[8]

My own experience in a drawing class taught with the Betty Edwards method confirms that anyone can learn to draw—and that we human beings are naturally equipped to capture what we see, if we are not too hampered by what we think we know, namely, that we cannot draw. What I and other students experienced as a result of her drawing class was improved concentration and visualization, problem-solving skills, shape discrimination, and of course, enhanced self-esteem.

Coming from a family of visual artists, two with bachelor of arts degrees, and a mother of great artistic talent, I directed my gifts into music and other hand arts that served me well from an early age to the present. I did not venture into areas already "taken" by three siblings, and I dared not call myself an artist. When I did gather up the courage to dabble in representational art, I quickly saw that I did not know the alphabet or the language. I concluded that I could not draw, never knowing that simple rudiments could help me with my skills.

Drawing is a language, potentially as important as reading and capable of framing a problem for new insights.

What the Betty Edwards method taught me fifty years later was that any of us can transfer what we see to paper in varying degrees of skill; but we need the same tools that help us read and write, hit a ball, or drive a car. We deny our gifts and beat ourselves up in certain arenas before we have learned the ABC's that help us translate our desire into results. I did capture my own hand and foot on paper in a recognizable way—the lines, the lumps, the veins, and all. My piano fingers that practiced endless scales and arpeggios took on a beauty of their own as I followed each thin track with the pencil until slowly, and painstakingly, my own hand emerged from the multiple erasures and smudges of a beginner. Bliss...Awe...Euphoria ...Ecstasy.

While drawing in the classroom with other blocked and untutored visual artists, I remembered my mother's portrait work from live models and her total absorption as she captured the character of certain faces and the pleasure she took in the artistic study of the human body. Somehow her hand of my childhood guided my tentative adult movements as I learned the alphabet of drawing. (My own No. 2 penciled body parts are now framed and hung with a newly born pride.)

Direct and intuitive knowing can be learned with spiritual teachers and mentors who value the presence of mystery in each of us, who aid our search for meaning and harmony, who deepen our awareness of how a paradigm shifts, how frustration and struggle precede insights, who celebrate the journey as well as the arrival. This may be the time to walk with a spiritual guide who will go with us to the edge where our peace is disturbed, while providing the security to risk flying. Guillaume Apollinaire, French poet and philosopher, put it this way:

Come to the edge, he said.
They said: We are afraid.
Come to the edge, he said.
They came.
He pushed them—and they flew.

Direct and intuitive knowing can be learned with spiritual teachers and mentors who value the presence of mystery in each of us.

Pathways to the Soul

Creative expression can be practiced in such a way that it becomes a spiritual exercise that leads us to communion with Christ. Some artists pray before they begin their work, putting themselves in the hands of Christ, asking for guidance and inspiration that others may see Christ's spirit in their work. Others light candles, pump iron, wear certain clothes or symbols, or wear nothing, listen to music, run a mile before tuning the cello. My own creativity covenant group that met for two and a half years prayed at the beginning of our sessions an edited version of the artist's prayer of Julia Cameron's book, *The Artist's Way.*[9] This doesn't mean that we have to burden ourselves with ritual or rules, perfection or stifling seriousness, even though we may set a certain tone or environment when we begin a creative assignment. Whatever stirs our creative juices is what's needed.

The landscape of our spirit is more apt to draw us into its own creative terrain when we give ourselves permission to be a beginner every day. We can remind ourselves it's OK to be an adult in the first grade of Creativity 101, or The Way of the Soul, Part II, in spite of the cultural pressure to know everything full-blown in adulthood. We do not have to be accomplished in things of the Spirit, or in things of child rearing, or love making, or prayer making.

Besides, Jesus sent the Holy Spirit for the very task of teaching us that the way of the spirit is not measured by accomplishment but by spirit. We have divine permission to be clumsy without embarrassment, awkward without apology, imperfect with acceptance, and childlike with wonder, while we delight in the adventure of spiritual play with an openness to new learning and exploration.

80

The pathways to learning the ways of the soul are many. Some seekers are attracted by the inner way of meditation, yoga, contemplation, biofeedback, chanting, creative prayer. Others choose the more active path of the outer way to learn the soul's terrain: service, acts of justice and mercy, advocacy, prophetic deeds, creative acts. However we respond to Christ's call we must bring our creativity along with us. Without it we are not whole and respond only with a partial self. The gift we have been given in Christ Jesus requires nothing less than the totality of who we are in the image of a creating God. No response is complete without the whole body, whole mind, whole spirit, and whole gifts, all in service to God, which bring us closer to the way of Christ and God's eternal vision.

Reflections and Activities

1. A commonly used phrase is "God moves in mysterious ways." Do you find the voice of God speaking through the newspapers or a child mysterious or unusual? Find a recent newspaper and select three stories, ads, or comics that speak with God's voice. Share with your group and keep it in your notebook or journal.

2. Saying no is a difficulty that many of us share. How-To books, classes, and Twelve-Step programs are built on helping us say no without guilt or apology. Are you able to discern that no is the best response when you are being invited or wooed or pursued for something that seems good, but is not right for you? Share your discernment process.

3. We seldom talk about direct knowing, though most of us have experienced it many times. In your study group list three encounters with direct knowing and share them. What are the similarities? the differences? Why is this a well-kept secret in the church and society?

4. Using the Betty Edwards chart of L-Mode and R-Mode, which is your preferred mental process? Does it change according to what you are doing? Does this match up with other inventories you have taken, such as Myers-Briggs, or others? Are you happy with what it says about you? How might you go about changing or strengthening your identified process?

5. Can you imagine discussing nightly dreams at your family table? Describe what it would be like. (No ridiculing allowed.) What might be the response on your job? in a small group? in an adult church school class? Name three dreams from the Bible. Research the Scriptures to find others and how they were used in God's plan. What might we gain if we took time to share our dreams?

6. Where have you gained new skill or grown creatively by following the nudge of direct knowing? Is this something you are proud of? How have you affirmed this new experience? Share in your group the importance of affirming our direct knowing and its importance in our lives.

7. What do you believe are the barriers to exploring direct knowledge in our faith communities? What could you do to break down or work around those barriers?

CHAPTER 6

Art Is Faith in Action

*A*rtists of every generation (that's all of us) join the Creator in telling the greatest story of the ages: God paints with crooked lines. Our creativity is the paintbrush God uses to shape the world day by day, saint by saint. Art is our faith in action. However, artists of every generation tell us there are days, even months and years, when faith is hard to sustain; and our creativity suffers from neglect, even abuse. These sages know from experience that these fallow times are not signals to give up on our dreams or to doubt the meaning of our work. Our own creative contributions are crucial for presenting God's story in its full potency. The very "stuff" of our lives—the chaos, the pain, the joy, the righteous anger—speaks, even screams, from the crucible of our faith, through our creative gifts.

"I don't know what it is but there's something spiritual about this piece," says a viewer who gently touches a certain art form. "This short story inspires me to make a real difference in the world," says a reader. We too, may find ourselves weeping, without knowing why, as we listen to a piece of music for the first time. The spiritual depths that we touch through the honesty of creativity that springs from our particular journey of faith interacts with the spirit in others, and by the miracle of grace, the sacrament of their lives and our lives is connected, crooked lines and all.

Addressing Our Pain

The painting and writings of Nora King, known for their power to motivate political action and justice, took a decidedly different turn when they became the channel of healing for her own pain. "When I recovered my full memory of being molested by an interviewing pastor for a youth summer program, my art changed from large canvas work with bold stokes to 12-inch square drawings. These were my private conversations about the abuse that happened to me. I would approach the canvas and just let my feelings dictate what I should paint. I found myself using lyric strokes and fluid movements—it just poured out of me. I painted with the emotions that were locked away before I faced the abuse—organic, connected, and flowing—the way life should be. Watercolor became my new medium so that I could put on layers of water to express the peace I wanted so desperately in my life and in the world. Over time my family and friends saw the calm that came over me when I painted. It was reflected in other arenas of my life also. I am still very much involved in the struggle for human rights, but it comes from a different place now. My hope and healing show in the bread I bake at 4 A.M....; it shows in reconnecting with nature— hanging clothes outside on a line. There's a reverence for simple things . . . that's important to me. I'm guided by the spiritual element of politics now, and my art reflects a centering that comes from widening solidarity to encompass solidarity with myself. Jesus is a comfortable citizen in all incarnations of justice, rising well above the limits of his followers. My present human rights work flows out of my childhood

84

love of the Jesus who defined modern human rights. Now I am more complete and can extend compassion more fully to my daughters and myself. My art helped get me to this point."[1]

We hasten the healing of our own deep wounds on the palette of pain, creativity, and faith. Much like the art of chiropractic, we knead and knuckle the memory of the hurt in our lives and in the world so that we may bring them to the surface and the healing light of Christ's reconciling power.

Although we may be tempted to dismiss their importance, or treat them as "just a hobby," or "my weekend sanity," our creative gifts are worthy of doxology on the altar of thanksgiving and vital to the meaning of our existence. "When the artist is alive in any person, he becomes an inventive, searching, daring, self-expressive creature," says Robert Henri. "He becomes interesting to other people. He disturbs, upsets, enlightens, and he opens a way for a better understanding."[2]

Our creative gifts are worthy of doxology on the altar of thanksgiving.

The precious life that is restored in ourselves and in others through these gifts, is a testament to Christ and the mysterious artistry of God's grace. Our talents contribute to the stream of hope and knowledge that inspire future generations. Our talents continue the conversation of creativity that began long before we entered the dialogue.

Our contribution feeds the lake, according to Madeleine L'Engle: "To feed the lake is to serve, to be a servant. . . . I have never served a work as it ought to be served; my little trickle adds hardly a drop of water to the lake, and yet it doesn't matter; there is no trickle too small."[3]

85

Embracing the Spiritual Struggle

The dialogue of faith and art does not promise to be tranquil or predictable. At times the interaction with the Spirit will be disturbing, disorderly, surprising, even destabilizing. The biblical examples of divine dialogue show us the risks of uncertainty and inner struggle that often accompany a core change of orientation, a new vision. Jacob's blessing did not come without bodily injury after turbulent wrestling with God the whole night long (Genesis 32:22-32). Paul's life turned 180 degrees after he was physically disabled, lost his sight, and neither ate nor drank for three days following his visitation by the Christ (Acts 9:1-9). The woman who met Jesus at the well reversed her life's direction after their intense interaction (John 4:1-30).

Though these stories of fearful or startling encounter with the divine may disturb our complacency or misdirected gifts, they offer us a handle on the spiritual struggle that permits us to grapple with God for the sake of our soul. The risk to our creativity and a settled faith is not that we will be disabled, but that we will be different from who we know ourselves to be. The loss of equilibrium that accompanies the spiritual struggle is temporary, as was Paul's three-day fast. But the risk of losing the artistic companionship of God is more devastating than the short-term instability of new birth.

Artists in Relationship

The creative process is not complete until it enters into relationship. The finished work is only the beginning. Our gifts have the potential to birth meaningful relationships beyond our imaginings.

Stained-glass artist Minnietta Millard speaks again of this ongoing relationship. While cleaning up her tools and paraphernalia after the installation of a large stained-glass window in her church, Minnietta looked around and saw a woman crying as she stood before the finished window. "It was a very tender moment," Minnietta said. "It's not often that an artist is privileged to see the effect the art has once it has left your hands."[4]

The word *art* comes from the root word meaning "to join; to fit together." In this pure sense, we are all artists in relationship. We may not all be sculptors or singers, but we find ways to relate—to fit our lives together in resourceful and relational ways every day, often with great imagination in spite of formidable obstacles. Being creative is not easy work but it is daily work. Fitting and joining the stuff of daily living does not wait for inspiration or studio time. This work requires a commitment to keep life going, to hold on to the vision we have been given; it involves a greater responsibility than satisfying our personal selves only; and yet it begins in the self, in our home, in our work.

Creative acts of joining and fitting things together connect us to our communities and the people within them to each other, to find hope and to give hope. These are active ingredients of transformation, creating ways of fitting things together—remaking our world joint by joint, fitting by fitting, as the small connections unite to make a new whole.

Creativity's Larger Mission

Corita Kent taught her students at Immaculate Heart College that creativity has a larger mission. "In a way, the maker (artist) gives us a small taste of the larger art—the new world we are trying to build—a world in which each person, each country, lives in harmonious relationship with each other person and country."[5]

We do not know in advance how God will speak through us or what of our talent will be required. What we can believe is that our gifts have the potential to make visible some facet of Jesus' ministry and his person—prophet, priest, and shepherd. Perhaps his healing ministry, giving voice to the voiceless, unburdening the oppressed, overcoming evil; his humor; his passion for living or proclaiming the gospel, will be made visible in some fashion through our creative making and doing.

Our gifts have the potential to make visible some facet of Jesus' ministry and his person—prophet, priest, and shepherd.

There are times when our highly personal acts of creativity are transformed by the Spirit into agents of prophetic action with the power to affect more broadly the lives of many people. These acts might even be viewed as forerunner acts, like John the Baptist, preaching a gospel of baptism and repentance that pointed to Jesus.

This prophetic and compassionate ministry of preparation can be seen in the stages of the NAMES Project that began with the simple act of one person containing his grief in a remnant of cloth that spelled out his friend's name. Soon others in bereavement made their remnants and joined them together. Over many months more pieces were made and individual panels of cloth were sewn together, offering mutual healing and acceptance, a place to share the loss. These simple acts of love were the beginning of prophetic action, legislation, public drama, and radical acts of faith that came—stitch by stitch, tear by tear. The AIDS Memorial Quilt has changed the world, bit by bit, binding together beyond time and space millions of kindred travelers who have lost loved ones to AIDS.

Taking a cue from the prophets of God, the traveling display of the AIDS Memorial Quilt is a kind of intense street theater, albeit performed in silence, that confronts prevailing notions about disease and lifestyle with a new social order of hospitality and justice. Much like the prophets of old who dramatized their radical message from God with actions that shocked their audience using dramatic costume and extreme speech, the reality of the traveling quilt arrests the comfort zone of its audience and reaches beyond the convention of the day. The art of the needle, an age-old female pastime, still pierces the heart of the world at a depth where only Spirit can reach.[6]

The Spirit Intercedes

When "we do not know how to pray," writes Paul in Romans 8:26, "the Spirit helps us in our weakness" and "intercedes with sighs too deep for words." The Spirit intervenes for us, as John Taylor points out in *The Go-Between God*, making us aware of the "heartbreaking brutality and the equally heartbreaking beauty of the world. . . . The Holy Spirit is that power which opens eyes that are closed, hearts that are unaware and minds that shrink from too much reality."[7] This dynamic Spirit creates an environment for our creative gifts to reveal the judgment and the promise of prophetic action that confronts the brutality in our world with a new compassion.

When we take our gifts into the public sphere, wherever that public is for us, we proclaim to others and to ourselves, "I trust"; "I believe"; "I am vulnerable."

"I trust" that these gifts contribute to the holy art of living.

"I believe" that I am not alone, as I have seen to the depth.

"I trust" that this creative gift will connect soul to soul.

"I believe" that the Holy Spirit will facilitate the dialogue through this creative doing.

"I am vulnerable" to being known at the core of my being.

Showing Our Creativity "in Public"

The marketplace for our souls demands the best of our creative gifts to rescue us from apathy and to animate our vision of a new horizon. In the business district where I travel every day on the way to my place of ministry, I frequently drive behind a brightly painted bus that generates a morning smile despite the state of the world on any given day.

Laughing back at me and the community of co-travelers are the characters of Miss Robinette's third-grade class project. They are known by their corkscrew hair and primary color clothes, their button eyes, and long skinny arms that span the length of the colorful bus taking passengers throughout the area. Chalkboard letters broadcast these young artists, their teacher, and the "man" who helped them with their project. Looking up at these wacky, winsome playmates radiating joy into morning traffic, who could resist contemplating a brighter future?

90

When hope inhabits our shared spaces, it rushes through the holes in our comfortable public imagination like the mighty winds of Pentecost, jolting us with a new vocabulary for discovering who we are and who we might become. This revelatory function of creativity makes us visible to ourselves in forms that sneak past our censors, showing us our struggles, our truths, our heights, and our depths.

As practicing adults who continue to learn the value of nourishing the child within us, we have the obligation to integrate the creativity of children into the public arena. In that way they too may authenticate their visions for our world and participate in God's transformational process that celebrates their incredible uniqueness and the world as they know it.

The kinds of creativity we choose to display on the walls of our church social halls, our school corridors, our public parks, and our diverse galleries have the awesome potential to proclaim and visually create a different world where humanity and peace inhabit the same space. From street art that is costumed in dragons and flowers, to the public art that we stretch across the sky, we authenticate the power of creativity to lift us heavenward, to plummet us into fear, to show us our terror, and to turn us to good or ill. The energy that emanates from the creative process, though masked from naked eyes, is divine love that has been entrusted to us for the good of humankind and all created life.

The Lord Has Need of Them

As artists of God we cannot escape the stewardship of our gifts or the prophetic and priestly dimension of our creativity any more than we can deny Christ's call to be his followers. Whether we desire it or not, our creating is bound to the indwelling spirit of Christ's mission in the world. Our creative awareness may not have sprung from such lofty goals, but Christ has need of our abilities for infusing all that is with sacred beauty and the artistry of hope.

As daughters and sons who share God's nature, we also share in the gift-giving of God that births new realities through the unconditional giving of ourselves. Our artistry was designed for the glory of God. We can claim this pivotal phrase, "The Lord has need of it," as our liberating mantra, remembering the owner who gave up his colt for Jesus' triumphal ride into Jerusalem (Luke 19:29-35, RSV). The Lord has need of our gifts for significant purposes also. We have the power to inspire the ecstasy of priestly praise and prophetic action that breaks new ground for God's passion—a creative and peace-giving universe that mirrors the heart of God.

This unconditional giving of our self, with all its creative gifts, is not without obstacles and challenges as we grow into the *Imago Dei*—the image of God—we were made to be. Who of us knows what will be required of us as we seek to be both faithful and creative.

Rollo May, in *The Courage to Create,* wrote: "To live into the future means to leap into the unknown, and this requires a degree of courage for which there is no immediate precedent and which few people realize."[8]

A Game Born of God

Rhea Zakich, devoted follower of Christ in a United Methodist Church and creator of the "UNGAME," knows well the courage that we struggle for and the Spirit's constant labor to birth God's creative power in us, despite overwhelming emptiness and despair. "I had no clue what I was doing. I had become mute and was enclosed in a silent tomb that cut me off from the world I was a part of in so many ways. Even my church and my family did not know how to relate to me when I couldn't talk." Rhea's surgeon had removed tumors from her vocal cords and by accidentally cutting too much, imposed long months of external silence for their healing. "With my voice gone I felt like a zero. I didn't know if I would ever speak again. The isolation was incredible."

One morning Rhea cried out in desperation and agonizing prayer, emptying all her grief and exhaustion into God's hands asking, "'How am I going to have a life?'" "Though I'd been aware of God's presence through this ordeal I was really asking if God would still be with me, whatever the future held. In the quiet of my kitchen I took out the drawing pad which had become my close companion and began to make curved lines—sort of like a road that meandered across the page, a road of life, I thought. Wonderings and questions came to me. What would I ask people if I could talk? What would I want them to ask me? The more I wrote, the more the questions poured out. Two hours later I stopped writing and stacked two hundred note cards on the drawing pad."

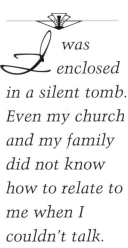

I was enclosed in a silent tomb. Even my church and my family did not know how to relate to me when I couldn't talk.

Rhea's two boys saw her doodlings when they came home from school. "What's this, a game?" they asked. After dinner she played "the game" with her family. "We discovered more about each other in twenty minutes than we'd known in twelve years."

For the next few months Rhea constructed over one hundred roads with questions for neighbors, teachers, youth leaders, and church members, as people discovered they could talk about feelings without embarrassment in a noncompetitive way. It was a game but not a game; a win-win kind of sharing—there were no wrong answers and everybody came out a winner.

People dis-covered they could talk about feelings without embar-rassment in a noncompetitive way.

"I was inspired to send my hand-made prototype to game companies, but they wouldn't publish it because they saw no market for a noncompetitive game about values and feelings." Rhea collected stacks of rejection slips until a neighbor boy found one of her soiled homemade games in the trash one day. He took it home to his parents who saw the potential in her "reject" and eventually invested their life savings to start the UNGAME Company (now known as Talicor, Inc.) with Rhea's help. Two and one half million sales and twenty-five years later, Rhea still gets letters from people in prisons, hospitals, schools, and counseling centers whose lives have been changed through the UNGAME of God.

"I know this was born of God," says Rhea. "It came to me from the Spirit when I was at the lowest point in my life, limited by a lack of speech and cut off from everything that had given me meaning. I guess I was more available and receptive in my desperation. I discovered that down under all my pain and fear that I poured out to God was a wellspring of creativity I didn't know was there. Today I try to keep the channel open so I can be used for Christ."[9]

94

The more the passion of God fills our creative expression, the more our creativity itself will be transformed. Keeping the channel open will bring about changes we never imagined, yet they will enliven our spirit and convey to us God's joy. We will know through inner and outer confirmation that God is involved for our highest good and the greater good of the world we share.

Reflections and Activities

1. What is your experience of "God's crooked lines"?

2. Describe your experience of being in the presence of creative expression that is sacred or spiritual.

3. Research or invite an art therapist to speak to your group about the uses of art to redirect our life.

4. How might we treat our own creativity differently if we took seriously the concept that God uses it to reach others?

5. Spend some time with the Jacob story in Genesis 32:22-32. Can we presume to demand a response from God? When have you wrestled with a problem until you felt answered by God? Can this struggle apply to our creative talents? Are you wrestling with God right now about a significant issue in your life? Make a symbol that expresses your struggle.

6. Where do you see examples of joining and fitting

life together in spite of formidable obstacles? Is this an art?

7. Take time to observe the art in the public space where you travel. Does it inspire you? What would you change, add, delete? Find out who makes the decisions about visual art in your area. Can you have a say in this?

8. Is children's creativity displayed in your church? How might you go about affirming their expressions of creativity?

9. "The Lord has need of it" released transportation for Jesus. Fill in this sentence five times with your different creative talents.

   ✳ The Lord has need of my _____.

   ✳ The Lord has need of my _____.

   ✳ The Lord has need of my _____.

   ✳ The Lord has need of my _____.

   ✳ The Lord has need of my _____.

10. "How am I going to have a life?" was Rhea's desperate question of God. When (and where) have you felt deep despair—and your cry was heard by God? Record your experience or share it with a trusted companion.

CHAPTER 7

Seeing in the Dark

*L*earning to see in the dark is an apprenticeship the artist within us must serve if we are to accompany the God who inhabits all places. Adjusting our eyes to the darkness is more than a biological process of waiting for the pupils to dilate to the loss of light. This is an inner adjustment of unlearning the traditional meaning of darkness that pervades our Western civilization and mythologies. Adjusting our eyes to the darkness means remembering our origins and embracing the darkness as a friend to commune with. The friendliness of light we already know well. Most of us link the dark to negative feelings of fear, terror, death, and uncertainty, associations that have been imposed on the dark by we humans, who have learned to love the light and repel the dark.

A wider reading of myth, culture, and the Spirit reveals meanings of darkness that hold it sacred and vital to our spiritual journey. The theme of underworld journeys that unite a hero or a people to their soul is repeated in a multiplicity of cultural sagas. The "Underground Railroad" describes the heroic passage to freedom of black slaves in this country, a journey that reunited a people's soul and identity. Our own bodies need the dark to perform certain functions most efficiently, like the secretion of melatonin that is done when it's pitch black. In the darkness of the unknown, the dark of the womb, the dark of the dream world, the dark of the fertile earth—this is where birth, regeneration, soul synthesis, and new life is formed.

Our own Christian baptism, particularly by immersion, is a visceral symbol of darkness, dying with Christ, being plunged under the dark waters, and rising with Christ, a changed person. Transformation happens in the darkness of the water. As Christians we welcome this fundamental change. It happens in the promise of the dark.

Christian baptism, particularly by immersion, is a visceral symbol of darkness, dying with Christ, and rising with Christ, a changed person.

The God of the psalmist, who divided the darkness that covered the face of the deep, did not assign it to evil and the light to good; rather they are two manifestations of Creation, equally good in the sight of God.

> If I say, "Surely the darkness shall cover me;
>   and the light around me become night,"
> even the darkness is not dark to you;
>   the night is as bright as the day,
>   for darkness is as light to you.
>
> —Psalm 139:11-12

Seeing in the dark is an act of befriending, as we befriend the stars that illumine the dark. It can be as simple as closing our eyes and putting our imagination to work for us. It can be as planned as a guided meditation that leads us to different surroundings, to see with the eye of the mind, to pray, to picture new solutions to problems. Seeing in the dark is part of the essential structure of the true creative enterprise, like an arch or a keystone, not a bauble or an added decoration that we apply when it is finished.

Meeting God in the Dark

So what does it mean for the artist within us to see in the dark? Two examples will illumine this metaphor that connects us to imagination—our basic human ability that we use continually, often without thinking.

During a church visitation trip to Korea, our small group of travelers visited a prayer mountain retreat center in the city of Yoju. The mountain itself is a reclaimed gold mine that now draws hundreds of Korean Methodists from Kuro Central Church to regular prayer vigils and retreat gatherings.

As North American visitors to the mountain, we entered the cold, dark mouth of the cave not knowing how far we would trek through the dimly lit passage to reach the inner prayer chamber. We formed a chain of anxious seekers linked together hand-to-hand as we moved, heads bent over, through the narrow tunnel with its low stone ceiling. At length we emerged into a rock-hewn sanctuary, an enclosed space of immense mystery that seemed to echo the prayers and petitions from generations of Korea's people.

Our time of worship and Holy Communion was an experience of uniting with the God of all peoples, all mountains, all prayers and petitions, all histories and all futures. We felt the cloud of witnesses hover near: miners in the tunnel; indentured workers from the Occupation; prayer visionaries who crawled on their knees, risking danger, embracing the inner darkness of the mountain to carve out a chamber—a womb—for communing with God inside the fertile earth. Our souls were filled with awe.

Sometimes during prayer vigils, when *Tongsung Kido* is offered to God (simultaneous prayers spoken aloud by worshipers), all lights are extinguished to pierce the veil of time and space, symbolically uniting them to their forebears through prayers of confession and brokenness.

Seeing in the Dark

Reclaiming the dark as a potent and regenerative symbol of creative power is necessary for our creative unfolding and spiritual renewal. The meeting place with God is often in the dark. For our brother Paul it was the dark of his blindness; for Jacob, the dark night of his wrestling; for John of the Cross, it was the dark night of the soul.

To be sure, we are not abandoned in our search to meet God or in our efforts to embrace the dark. It is at these times that the manifestation of the Spirit is most palpable. The Holy Spirit, the Paraclete, the one who runs alongside, draws close to aid and assist our searching and our encounters. This Advocate acts as the "go-between God" that inhabits our dialogue in the dark and in the light. This divine relationship is tested and made stronger in the struggles of the soul.

Learning from the dark is not a lesson most of us would choose if given the choice. Sometimes it happens in spite of ourselves. Why try to see in the dark when we can see much better in the light? we ask. This was the question that twenty-two women asked in the small town of Pacific Grove, California, on the Monterey Bay, where the Monarch butterflies overwinter.

"Creative Visioning for Women"

Seeking to enhance creative vision, we were women from a variety of professions and pursuits who gathered together for a weekend of "seeing in the dark." The seminar was deceptively titled "Creative Visioning for Women."

Most of us were strangers to each other but very much alike in our shared need for fresh inspiration in our creative work and new ways to see our surroundings and ourselves. The brochure asked us to bring a scarf and a camera as tools for our work. We had no idea why the scarf was needed; but workshops like this are known for their enigmatic content, so we all brought scarves and extras for unexpected use. Each of us arrived with a crazy quilt of scarves and an impressive array of cameras; point and click, SLR's, and medium-format models.

On Saturday afternoon we were introduced to the mystery visioning assignment that would require our many-splendored scarves and our multi-manual cameras. Our artist/leader explained the task as we chose a partner for the assignment. For nearly an hour one of us wore our scarf, blindfold-style, and was slowly led by the hand throughout the rooms of the Art Center or down the stairs and onto the street where we were to make pictures. With our cameras in hand, we used the entire roll of film to "make pictures" in whatever environment our sighted partner chose for us, with only the slightest disclosure or description of the space we were in. After many minutes passed, or when we ran out of film, or stick-to-it-ive-ness, we switched roles so our partner could have the fun of taking pictures without the encumbrance of seeing.

101

Most of us were strangers to each other but very much alike in our shared need for fresh inspiration.

What is it like to be led by the hand in the dark with only a hint of your surroundings as you open and close the shutter of your camera? Click...click...click...click...twenty-four times...thirty-six shots.

What snaps in your head when you cannot see to focus your lens, position your subject, check your distance, choose your exposure, change your perspective, adjust for the light, turn your knobs, or just fiddle, and fiddle some more with the equipment, to punctuate the joy of seeing?

Our group returned from our excursions puzzled, worn out, wondering if it had been worth our effort, looking for answers to put our fragmented selves back together. As blindfolded photographers we described our journey: off balance, out of sync, disoriented, silly, out of control, foolish, awkward, uncoordinated, wasting time, dependent, uncreative, uncertain, afraid to risk, tired. As sighted guides we also felt a similar range of uninvited emotions: unneeded, protective, detached, playful, in control, mischievous, isolated, bored, ambivalent. On both sides of the lens our disorientation was exposed.

The instructor then asked us the pivotal question, "How many of you took your pictures holding the camera to your eye?" We all raised our hands together. "Why?" she asked. Before we could answer, I felt an epiphany coming around the corner to meet me. So did the others.

"You - couldn't - see - anything," she said slowly and deliberately. In the momentary silence that precipitated our burst of embarrassed laughter, we were suspended between the synapses of the brain, between knowing nothing and knowing everything. The same kind of light bulb goes off the first time a child "gets" a knock-knock joke—that split second before it all comes together in sweet and total recognition. It was as if we'd been struck by the proverbial bolt of lightning. "You could have held the camera anywhere and it would have worked just as well," she said, "on your head, at your knees, upside down, crooked, at your side."

A Fresh Look Through the Lens

In that moment of revelation we saw ourselves through a fresh lens—locked into the patterns of our past, creatures of artistic habit, stuck in our comfortable yesterdays. Everything about our environment had changed, yet we made our photos in the same dependable, predictable way. It didn't help, but we did it anyway. Even the college student on holiday from Germany was stuck in old perceptions. (I felt better.) She was my partner and her camera was at eye level too. Youth has no monopoly on unfettered thinking, although I did come away with a half roll of puzzling shots of swinging doors, marble tile, sinks, and commodes from our foray into the bathroom (ugh). She was very mischievous.

Were we stuck in our creative thinking? Yes!
Were we hampered by a spirit of fear? Yes!
Did we cherish our familiar patterns? Yes!
Was the darkness our enemy? Yes!

Even those who took pride in being risk takers—sideways thinkers, innovators—were reduced to safe looking, imprisoning their imagination, afraid to examine external restraints; and working dutifully within the box we were given.

The parable of the blindfold continues to haunt me and teach me. It draws my glance from heaven to earth, from earth to heaven like Jacob's ladder, creeping behind my eyes to tickle them to attention should they lapse into lethargy again, as they did in that small town brushed with butterfly dust.

Seeing Is More Than Looking

As artists of the Imago Dei, creative vulnerability is the apron we put on before we pick up our tools. It defines who we are and Whose we are—those who walk with a God who anchors us securely when our eyes turn to buttons and go blank in the dark. We are those for whom the Prayer of St. Patrick enfolds our making and doing:

> Christ be with me, Christ within me,
> Christ behind me, Christ before me,
> Christ beside me, Christ to win me,
> Christ to comfort and restore me,
> Christ beneath me, Christ above me.
> Christ in quiet, Christ in danger,
> Christ in hearts of all that love me,
> Christ in mouth of friend and stranger.[1]

Creativity that risks needs immersion in Jesus, the Friend of artists, for a new journey of trust.

Halford Luccock, in his book *In the Minister's Workshop*, describes the primacy of the imagination that transcends the eye in creating a visual picture.

104

"In seeing the world and people, the process is essentially a religious one, that of diminishing preoccupation with self. A mind at leisure from itself is the only one that has time to see." His chapter, "The Harvest of the Eye," cloaks the eye in transparent garments of hospitality and grace. "We never really see the world or other people if our own figure is always in front of us blocking the view."[2]

Our workshop assignment was a mirror that reflected an undiminishing preoccupation with self that prevented us from hearing, touching, and sensing the friendly potential of our environment. "Preoccupation with self is the greatest barrier to seeing, and the hardest one to break," says Freeman Patterson in *Photography and the Art of Seeing*.[3] To an outsider it would appear that our seeing was blocked by a colorful blindfold; but we learned that the primacy of our comfort, our familiar patterns, our safety, our product, our image, was the log in our eye. The darkness was the friend we took for granted because it stood so close.

Seeing is more than looking. Those among us who practice different methods of seeing, out of necessity, know that we can "see" with our ears, our hands, our smell, our touch. This inner eye of the heart is what Jesus meant when he said, "Do you have eyes, and fail to see? Do you have ears, and fail to hear?" (Mark 8:18). "Let anyone with ears to hear listen" (Mark 4:9, 23).

Click...click.

Famous Amos of packaged cookie

Seeing is more than looking. Those who practice different methods of seeing, out of necessity, know that we can "see" with our ears, our hands, our smell, our touch.

105

fame didn't achieve peace of mind or a piece of his financial future until he made cookies from his "inner chef." "I AM THE COOKIE" is his personal motto that shapes cookie dough from the heart.[4] This capacity to merge with our subject or task, becoming the "other" that we paint, or teach, sing, cook, compose, or love, is the essence of spiritual teachings and good coaching in many disciplines. The inner game of tennis, golf, running, swimming, all preach the cultivation of the inner eye.

In *Zen Seeing, Zen Drawing*, artist Frederick Franck draws us onto a crowded New York street where his eye follows a man in the crowd whom he might have processed as for a police report: "male, sixtyish, white, poor, limping, decrepit." When an image goes through the arc of the heart and not simply through the computer-brain, as Franck insists it must for compassionate, creative seeing, we relate at a deeper level. "I had 'become' him, had been a child with him, a cocksure adolescent. I had grown old, worn out with him. His feet were killing me."[5] This awakening to the communication from heart to heart is what pours out through our creative work to show the mystery and grandeur of God's creation. The miracle of our imagination is that we can use it blindfolded. We who function with the sight of our eyes have many journeys yet to make on the road to risk and exploration, trust and intimacy with the environment, as we learn to see more in the dark.

The paradox of seeing in the dark is that we must shift our gaze to see the light that comes from struggling in the dark to see the light.

Click ... click. ...

Accepting the Risk

We cannot escape the risk that walks hand in hand with the creative process. Creative people are not afraid to walk two steps, or more, into the darkness, the unknown. "Creative people are committed to risk," says Benny Golson, jazz musician and composer. "Everybody can see what's in the light. They can imitate it, they can underscore it, they can modify it, they can reshape it. But the real heroes delve in darkness of the unknown....And many times that's the way our ideas are, the ones we create from darkness. Darkness is important—and the risk that goes along with it."[6]

"Open my eyes, that I may see...."

Click...Click...Click.

Reflections and Activities

1. What are your earliest memories of the dark? Share these with your group or a friend.

2. Research some mythologies and other cultural stories that use darkness as a part of the journey for wholeness or completion to occur. Find one story from your own culture of origin.

3. With what do we associate darkness in this country? Are there any problems with these connections? How might we go about changing or reclaiming the darkness as a positive symbol?

4. What are some ways dark and light are used in

Scripture? What does this say to you? Do some study on these passages and share with your group.

5. Have you ever been blindfolded? in a game? What was your experience like?

6. Take some time and find out what it is like to live without eyesight by talking with someone who is blind or partially sighted. Hear with your heart. Seek to learn how he express himself creatively. What are her joys and frustrations?

7. Where are you willing to risk new creativity? How will you get started? Find a companion to make yourself accountable to in this new step. Check in weekly.

CHAPTER 8

Past Watchful Dragons

C. S. Lewis was a lover of fairy tales. As a child he would read them voraciously while savoring every hero's deed through mythic lands with colorful characters. Lewis credits fairy tales with "baptizing" his imagination. "When I was ten" said Lewis, "I read fairy tales in secret and would have been ashamed if I had been found doing so. Now [that was in 1952] that I am fifty, I read them openly. When I became a man I put away childish things, including the fear of childishness and the desire to be very grown up."[1]

Lewis employed a favorite tool of illusion to communicate the eternal realities that he experienced in his conversion from atheism to the Christian faith. He knew from childhood how a frozen imagination could impede the power of the gospel to woo us into its spell, so he set out to cast it in a form that broke with the tradition of his day. Lewis's own explanation of why the *Chronicles of Narnia* were written in the fairy tale genre leads us to consider the intimidating gaze of our own "watchful dragons."

> I thought I saw how stories of this kind could steal past a certain inhibition which had paralysed much of my own religion in childhood. Why did one find it so hard to feel as one was told one ought to feel about God or about the sufferings of Christ? I thought the

chief reason was that one was told one ought to. An obligation to feel can freeze feelings. And reverence itself did harm. The whole subject was associated with lowered voices; almost as if it were something medical. But supposing that by casting all these things into an imaginary world, stripping them of their stained-glass and Sunday school associations, one could make them for the first time appear in their real potency? Could one not thus steal past those watchful dragons? I thought one could.[2]

The Chronicles of Narnia are gleeful proof that C. S. Lewis invented a new vehicle for transmitting the good news of Christ to young and old alike in a way that crosses all barriers in its appeal. The infectious characters of Aslan the Lion, Caspian, and the Pevensie children of the wardrobe closet make us glad that Lewis did not put away childish things when he became a man but said yes to the childhood of his heart and gave us the gospel through the eyes of children.

Rousing the Dragons

Are there dragons we might rouse when we give free reign to our imagination? You bet there are! Must we tiptoe beyond a watchful past that guards our creative approach to things dear to our heart? Can we keep the dragons at bay—or at the very least transform them into friendly creatures, such as Puff, the magic dragon, or Barney, friend of children? You bet we can! We must train ourselves to recognize dragons when we see them. Granted, not every dragon is fierce and fire-breathing. In fact, not all dragons look alike, even at night.

110

The task of the creative traveler is to know an unfriendly dragon when we see one; to determine whether it has the ability to attack and swallow our creativity whole and to discern if it can be subdued with our best menacing growl; a swish of the sword; and a cocky, confident walk. The proper "dragon-scare" weapons are crucial to sustaining our creative freedom.

Lessons in Dragon-ology

Here are ten easy lessons in dragon-ology, complete with their guiding principles and fire-laden vocabulary. Dragons are known to hide under the moat called "The Believable Truth." You will know them by their long sentences that sound suspiciously like acceptable truth. I have included moat-crossing strategies for getting to the other side unsinged in spite of their nostrils of fire, lashing tails, and stickery scales.

The **DRAGON** of **AGE**

Dragon Fire: Slow down when you hit seventy, because you're now a bona fide septuagenarian. Sixty is not too early to reduce your speed either...after all, you're a sexygenarian...oops, a sexagenarian!

Dragon Talk: Now that you're older you should be more careful, accept poor health, give up creative pursuits, sleep more, eat less, live closer to your children.

Crossing the Moat: A seventy-eight-year old woman was a faithful member of my class in "Faith and Creative Arts," which inspired her to action. In response to the Feedback Questionnaire she wrote: "My next creative step is making contact with the Center for the Partially Sighted. Since I lost control of

111

my vision, I was unsure about my ability to continue creative writing. With their help I will soon have a computer device that should help me return to my writing letters and devotional talks." The octogenarians I know can't find enough time to do all the things they'd like to do. An anonymous author says that "life begins at eighty. After all, it's a succession of birthday parties."

The **DRAGON** of **TITLE**

Dragon Fire: Don't call yourself an artist.

Dragon Talk: Real artists work hard at their craft for many years; pay money for schooling; and have certificates, lots of sales, business accounts, and patrons to prove they're worthy of the title. People will think you're a braggart, feeding your ego, puffing yourself up. Besides, God blesses the meek.

Crossing the Moat: A retired pastor has been working in wood for fifty years, giving away his beautiful hand-carved crosses as gifts and mementos of special occasions. In his hands wood sings. After many years of shaping, honing, planing, and loving the wood he carves, he now calls it his art. Long before he began using the word *artist* to describe his work, other people saw the artistry of his craft and applied the title to him. Now that he's retired he sometimes uses *artist* about himself.

The word *artist* comes from the same root word that means "the joining and fitting" we do every day that brings things together in new ways and makes something unique. In this sense we are all artists. We need not wait to have the title conferred by a certificate or degree. Create your own official title. Put it on your refrigerator door, your license plate, your office door, your lunch box: Artist / Engineer, Artist /

Gardener, Artist / Father, Artist / Artist, Artist / Cook, Artist / Punster, Artist / Videographer, Artist / Birdwatcher, Artist / Librarian, Artist / Babysitter, Artist / Calligrapher, Artist / Bookkeeper, and so on. Jesus said to let your light shine.

The **DRAGON** of **Cookie Jar Etiquette**

Dragon Fire: If you play the flute, don't try to write poetry.

Dragon Talk: One gift per person, please. There are only enough cookies in the jar for one apiece. Don't be greedy!

Crossing the Moat: Where did we come up with the idea that God is stingy with creative gifts? Your fair share doesn't apply in this case, as creative gifts are not apportioned according to a set formula, like some church offerings that shall remain nameless. Bezalel, the artist for building the Tabernacle (Exodus 31:1-5), was gifted with a long list of artistic talents. Huram-abi, who directed the building of Solomon's Temple (2 Chronicles 2:13-14), is described as trained "to execute any design that may be assigned him." Both artists used all their abilities to teach and install the many specifications for the construction. God is "generous to a fault," and aren't we glad? (Hey, there are some cookies still in the jar!)

The **DRAGON** of **Timeliness**

Dragon Fire: Start your creative pursuits when you're young if you really want to be good and get the most value out of it.

Dragon Talk: We all know that it's tough to teach an old dog new tricks, so don't wait until you have a family and are burdened with responsibilities to find what makes you happy.

Crossing the Moat: Walt began piano lessons in his sixties. The community college classroom has five pianos and two people at each keyboard. Walt enjoys practicing late at night with earphones plugged into his full keyboard synthesizer. He adds the percussion button to most pieces. ("Für Elise" wired with snare drum—what would Beethoven say?)

Jan started ballet lessons when she was thirty. She's always wanted to learn and now enjoys using her mind and her muscles. God doesn't draw in the moat at mid-life. Why should we?

The **DRAGON** of **Consistency**

Dragon Fire: Don't switch horses in midstream.

Dragon Talk: Find one gift and perfect it. Settle down. If you jump around from one thing to another you won't be good at anything.

Crossing the Moat: After twenty-one years as a local church pastor, the Reverend Steve Goodier switched his ministry to a new venue. A United Methodist elder, Reverend Steve resigned his Denver, Colorado, church pulpit to expand his growing e-mail enterprise called "Your Life Support System." His uplifting spiritual messages reach 61,000 people in 100 countries, many who are churched and many who are self-proclaimed doubters and skeptics. It began as a part-time fun thing when his wife gave him a laptop computer for their twenty-fifth wedding anniversary in 1998. A few messages to friends and family have mushroomed into three self-published books of his popular e-mail messages, daily answers to incoming e-mail, and heavy research for updating the "life support" system.

Reverend Steve found that he could not pastor his church and keep up the business—so he chose to continue in cyberspace as an international spiritual counselor while his wife kept her day job. He describes his job change as "scary." He even had one child in college and another one right behind him at the time. Whew! That's tiptoeing on the *edge* of the moat!!

The **DRAGON** of **Appropriateness**

Dragon Fire: Act your age. Be serious.

Dragon Talk: The world doesn't need any more silliness. Leave foolishness to the kids and paid comics. What we need are clear-headed thinkers who can keep this world on track with rationality and logic.

Crossing the Moat: Every year thousands of people dress up as clowns and entertain children, delight adults, perform at parties, preach from the pulpit, fall off ladders, perform at the circus, attend clown school, march in parades, have a wonderful time, and bring us joy. The Pacific School of Religion in Berkeley, California, where they believe the arts help us find spiritual answers to religious questions, even has a summer Institute of the Arts that teaches clowning under the heading "Bringing to Life Biblical Humor." Mime, drama, and storytelling for worship are also in the summer curriculum. Clowning is serious business!

A pastor in Hawaii who collects funny stories and jokes published them (copy machine style) as *Alo'ha-Ha-Ha: Recycled Jokes in Paradise*. Here are some titles from the seventy joyful ticklers: "The Creation Committee," "A Lawyer's Prayer," "The Twenty-Third Pound," "The Legend of W.C."[3]

The **DRAGON** of **Past Mistakes**

Dragon Fire: Once you have made some really BIG mistakes, like the ones that land you in prison, there's

115

not much you can expect in the way of being creative. Your life is confined; so are your mind and spirit.

Dragon Talk: You have made your bed; now lie in it. Adults have to accept the consequences of what they do.

Crossing the Moat: The Bedford Hills Correctional Facility for Women has a writing program called "Life Sentences—Sentences for Life." Prisoners are taught creative writing as a way to reclaim their lives, their past, their crimes, and their future. Their stories were read by well-known women in film and theater as a fund raiser for a women's college program. The writing program shows the profound spiritual search of the prison writers.

The **DRAGON** of **"Real Artists"**

Dragon Fire: The marks of a legitimate artist are a public following, public presentations, and a body of work that makes money to live on full time. Real artists have real resumés that list the many galleries where their work has been shown individually, the sales to corporate headquarters, the overseas commissions, the write-ups, the table-top books, the openings, the awards, the publicists, the agents, the homes, the appearances, the tours, the interviews, the studio lofts, the blah, blah, blah. (Are my sour grapes smelling?)

Dragon Talk: A real artist is someone who is recognized by others as having a particular gift and who can do presentations or teach others to do the same thing—not like you.

Crossing the Moat: The Pacific Northwest Conference of The United Methodist Church published a collection of writing, music and art, prose and poetry, in a beautiful book titled *Qumran*. Invitations went out to churches for submissions to the publication, which were then juried by a committee for use in the anthology. Over sixty items were selected from the two hundred entries submitted for the premier issue. The creativity was presented in the spirit of the Qumran community near the Dead Sea where the scrolls of early believers were left behind in caves for the discovery of what they believed.

The **DRAGON** of **Physical Ability**

Dragon Fire: If you should not have the full use of every part of your body, then you cannot expect to be creative in the regular way. Be content with what can be salvaged and stay close to home in case you need physical assistance. In other words, color inside the lines.

Dragon Talk: Persons with physical and mental disabilities should not expect to achieve high creativity. When the interaction between mind, body, and spirit is impaired, the result will only bring frustration and further disappointment to someone who is already struggling against the odds.

Crossing the Moat: The Reverend Donna Fado Ivery was sitting in a restaurant when a two-hundred-pound glass partition fell from the ceiling and struck her on the head. For the next five years Donna suffered the sudden disability of chronic pain, mild traumatic brain injury, and cervical strain. The transition for her husband and two young children was also traumatic as the smallest tasks were now difficult—cooking, finding words to speak, seeing with double vision, maintaining continuity of thought.

"At the request of my therapist, I turned to painting to express myself," she recalled. "I started painting pictures of pain, a conversation between me and God."

117

Originally done for her own expression, Donna did not come to painting as an artist (one art class in college) but out of the need to express herself within the pain. "For every hour up I had to spend one hour in the bed. One up and one down."

Around the time of the third anniversary of her head and neck injury she began to see the image of dancing in her time of meditation, dancing with pain. Donna subsequently painted the image of herself dancing with pain using broken mirrors and oils. Poetry was also born through her suffering, prayer, and this meditation.

Dancing With Pain
> *I do not choose to have Pain as my Partner*
> > *following my every step*
> > *bending my body to its intention*
> > *holding me always with cutting arms*
> > *tripping me up to fall fully into its*
> *blunt, harsh body*
> > *reflecting distorted and exaggerated*
> *aspects of me*
> > *I do not choose to have Pain as my Partner*

The final stanzas of Donna's poem are a testament to hope:

> *It is a precarious, delicate dance I live*
> > *with this nasty Partner called Pain.*
> *But Pain knows and follows rhythm!*
> *Therefore, I choose to improve my dance*
> *acumen*
> > *I will*
> > > *outwit,*
> > > > *out step,*
> > > > > *out invent.*

118

I will keep up a joyous movement
while keeping in rhythm with life's music,
while keeping in rhythm with Pain.
Will I become so advanced, that I will take the lead?[4]

Donna's brochure, *Art of Healing*, shows some of her paintings and describes her healing journey workshops along with Spirit Brush Arts, the business she formed as a resource to others. With the help of a cane and an electric scooter, she travels the country (one trip a month) speaking to many diverse groups about the character of pain, faith, tears, and wholeness.

Are there other teachings that inhibit our gifts that might be considered watchful dragons? What about the writings of Scripture? Are there any watchful dragons there? Let's look at our cherished interpretations of certain passages to see if they inhibit our full use of God's generous gifts.

The **DRAGON** of **Fixed Gifts**

Dragon Fire: Spiritual gifts are the same yesterday, today, and for eternity.

Dragon Talk: You do not have the gifts named in the Bible, so your talents don't mean as much as others who know without a doubt that they are healers, preachers, teachers, and administrators.

Crossing the Moat: Gifts of the Spirit are not a closed chapter but a disclosure of what is yet to come. The primary texts for spiritual gifts are 1 Corinthians 12:4-11 and Ephesians 4:7-13. These chapters enumerate many gifts of the Spirit and their purpose in building up the church and witnessing to the unity of the Spirit. These spiritual gifts, or abilities, are frequently taught as the complete and final list of spiritual gifts, yet they are but a hint, an aperitif of what is in store

119

for us as God continues to re-create, refine, and redefine the gifts needed in every generation.

More on Spiritual Gifts

These foundational passages might be viewed as the opening act, like opening night at the theater. Patrons who have tickets for the middle of the run, or closing night, experience a more mature play, subtle or major changes, additions, subtractions from the original script, even replacement of actors. C. S. Lewis's favorite analogy goes even further to show us our smallness in the grand scheme of history: "We do not know the play. We do not even know whether we are in Act I or Act V. We do not know who are the major and who are the minor characters. The Author knows."[5]

We are still at opening night and the church is in its infancy. What we do know is that the church is of God and will last until the end of time; therefore we must be open to changes in definition and experience of Paul's compendium of God's revealed gifts for the church. Just as the prohibition against women speaking in the church and teaching men is now understood in the context of Paul's particular congregation and the culture at Corinth, we cannot apply it to women for all time. Likewise the full range of gifts themselves must be open to further revelation to embody the vision of God's reign in every age.

Many teachings on the spiritual gifts have not served the inclusiveness of Christ. Dedicated believers who cannot find their gifts and experience reflected through the particularity of Paul's gifts often feel excluded and unused in God's mission. What of our legitimate gifts that are not in these categories? In the next stage of Christian history many more people will come to the Christian faith with a new variety of gifts, and service, and working, that are not specifically contained in the particular grouping of 1 Corinthians 12 or Ephesians 4, although these gifts may come to them in time.

The more we affirm a wider diversity of gifts and talents as legitimate and spiritual resources for the common good, the more joy of the Spirit we will see in our church, our service, and our lives. In the act of blessing the abilities and talents we bring as spiritual gifts and recognizing that they are all from God, the church will experience a renewed expression of creativity that permeates our life in Christ at a deep and sustaining level. The gifts of the early church are significant, necessary, and ordained by God. They will serve us better if conceived as a foretaste of what is to come, an aperitif of continuing revelation that contributes to building the church until Jesus returns.

More Moat Crossing Tools

A little-known defense against dragons is the "two thumbs up" sign. This may appear to be giving them the "Go Ahead." To the contrary, it is a sign to ourselves that WE are not all thumbs. This sign of confidence has been known to drive dragons back into their lair because they sense our strength and power. If you sing a few lines about "Puff, The Magic Dragon" this helps too. (Go ahead—sing it.) As you make the thumbs up sign right now wherever you are, say these words of God's protection from Psalm 91:12-13: "They [angels] will carry you in their arms / in case you trip over a stone. / You will walk upon wild beast and adder, / you will trample young lions and snakes" (NJB). Now go for it—thumbs up—you have all the tools you need. Cross that moat!

Reflections and Activities

1. Make a quick list of "dragons" that keep you from exercising all of your creativity. Don't censor yourself—just do stream of consciousness writing.

2. Begin building your very own kit for "dragon bites." Which of the dragons is the most fearsome or troublesome for you? Why? Can you think back to earlier life experiences in which the dragon first appeared? What were the circumstances and how did you feel? What did you do? What do you need to minimize the fire of these dragons and start crossing the moat? What will you do when you get across the moat? What can you do to prevent the dragons from reappearing?

3. Name the travelers you want to go with you as you make this "moat" journey. Include the qualities they have that you need.

4. What gift can you give yourself for making this "dangerous" journey? Be generous with yourself.

5. You may now declare your dragons extinct. So be it! What kind of freedom does this provide? Create a way to celebrate your new freedom and share it with a friend.

CHAPTER 9

What the Church Can Do

*E*very Sunday of the year the foyer at La Mesa United Methodist Church in San Diego is bustling with activity as members rush to the newest "Prayers and Squares" quilts. Members circle the quilts like a fish feeding frenzy to tie a prayer knot into the colorful squares of cloth that will soon leave the church as completed gifts. Each person knows that his or her love knots are part of the finishing touch that stamps each quilt "Ready for Delivery." In the past two years three hundred quilts have been sent to persons in need throughout San Diego County and to other states by a group that has become known as the Prayer Quilter's ministry, a group of fifteen to twenty-five persons, mostly women.

These lap quilts are visible to everyone as they hang from a quilt rack. During worship the receiver's name and prayer need are read and included in congregational prayers of the morning. The pastors carry out the quilts, "following the light," where the personal knots are tied with prayer. Two hundred children in vacation Bible school helped design quilts for children. Everybody has a part in completing these handmade quilts, gifts of love that say to people in crisis, "You are not alone; we believe in God's power to comfort, strengthen, and heal." The final touch is a personalized label: *This is made especially for (recipient's name); Sewn in love all over.*

La Mesa church is part of the interdenominational outreach ministry started by Hope UMC of San Diego in 1992 by quilters with no other purpose than to have fun together. They now have amazing stories of healing and recovery from persons who have been nurtured by this creative ministry. Like Bible study, mission outreach, and acts of peace and justice, Prayers and Squares shows us that our creativity is not, strictly speaking, a private act. It is rooted in community and shows the eternal in the here and now.

Learning by Heart, Playing by Ear

These stories of what churches do to sew, paint, and craft creativity into the life of faith are multiplied over and over again as the church participants discover new ways to reach out through their gifts and talents to bring hope to others. How might God's gift of creativity be a part of everything we do in and through our churches, from Bible study to community outreach to youth car washes? Would things look different if we purposely infused our faith with the creativity factor?

How about naming an artist in residence for the church the way we do for a scholar, or writer, or musician in residence at a college or university? Could we help support an endowed chair for Creativity and Faith at a nearby seminary? Would we not witness to God's larger beauty and the gifts of creation in all of us through this intentional outreach to the creative arts?

124

More Than Fluff

We in the church are rather timid about including the creativity of our work and our leisure as part of our calling to be Christ's disciples in the world. A person in one of my seminars asked, *"Isn't there a danger of going overboard with this creativity thing?"* The sincere concern behind this question is that the fundamental work of the church has nothing do with this *art thing.* His question is mirrored in the lack of attention we give to creative gifts in the church. We expect to see creativity in children's activities, vacation Bible school, youth fund-raisers, and the women's bazaar, and rightly so. But they cannot act as our surrogates in the realm of creativity. We are each given a measure of grace that assures us of the gifts of God in us; gifts of power to transform God's world.

The sisters of St. Joseph of La Grange have written a vision statement that guides their full-time work in the ministry of the arts.

> As Sisters of St. Joseph we encourage and affirm creativity in ourselves and all persons. Our mission of unity brings us in our time to a deeper awareness of our communion with God and all creation.
>
> Through the arts we contemplate and express the unity and holiness of all creation, and the heights and depths of the human heart in response to the great mysteries of existence. We affirm the power and prophecy of the arts and believe the arts to be an important ministry for hope and healing in a critical moment of world transformation.[1]

125

Baptizing Our Gifts

When our creativity is accepted in the church as a gift from God, it is symbolically baptized; and the hand of blessing rests on our natural creative gifts and deems them deeply significant to God. We are released for deep joy. We know that our creative gifts are sacred; and the doing that gives us great joy, gives great joy to God also. What more could we want?

This baptism of our gifts is the work of the church. No other institution, or persons, or organization can do what the church can do in this way. No award ceremony, no public recognition, no gold watch can touch the depths of our being as can the body of Christ who marries our creative talents to Christ's sacred body. This is our calling as the church—to so infuse our gifts with Christ's presence that we are marked as artists for God.

The heart of the vision statement of the sisters of St. Joseph touches the core of creativity's purpose, "to bring us . . . to a deeper awareness of our communion with God and all creation." This high purpose should enrich and infuse everything that we do in the church. How often does someone ask if we are in danger of overdoing our finance committee meetings, community outreach, mission work, evangelism, or men's meetings, advocacy? In many ways, we in the church have abdicated what was born in our genesis and adopted a cultural definition of creativity that sidelines it to the perimeter of our lives as "entertainment," "fluff," "women's and children's work—transitory, cute, and irrelevant." Like a taxidermist's prize specimen, our creative gifts adorn our walls as reminders of their former virility and power but now

126

stare from their impotent perch with neither power nor pride.

We have forgotten that our creative gifts have the power to transform the world. They are viewed as a right-brain, intuitive mish-mash that have no internal structure and hence are without permanent value. Thus, architects are more valued than artists, scientists are seen as more important than sculptors, bridge builders as more needed than band teachers, doctors as better than dancers, and the list goes on. And yet it is the artists of day-to-day creativity that dare to make art because God is in art.

The question posed in my seminar helps us look again at our erroneous belief that creativity is something lightweight that we carry around in our pocket, like loose change, should an offering plate be passed unexpectedly, rather than as an integral and substantial component of our spiritual life. The notion that our ministry includes our creative gifts, or that our ministry *is* our creativity, is stepping into an area of uncharted waters for most people of faith, even for those who use their creative gifts in full-time professions in the church and community.

Every Place Has Its Gift to Offer

One area church established a relationship with the music department of the local high school as part of its partnership with the community. During the Christmas season the orchestral students walked eight blocks to the church carrying tubas, trumpets, violins, and other instruments not meant to be carried long distances, to present a program of seasonal music to members of the church, the adult school housed in the church, and community residents. Even the lack of money for a school bus did not prevent them from sharing the music they had practiced and perfected for the season. What else can the church do to foster creativity among its members and the community?

A downtown Lutheran church offers the hardwood floors in its large fellowship hall for ballroom dance classes four times a week. Over eighty-five people from beginner to advanced show up for cha-cha, east and west coast swing, tango, line dance, waltz, jitterbug, even salsa. I can personally attest to the creative sweat worked up by couples inside the walls of that church where the music is salty and sweet and the spirit of sacred celebration permeates the space.

Celebrating Our Gifts

How does your church proclaim the message that Jesus celebrated the art of a wedding? Is there an air of "get-down-boogie" anywhere in your activities, or is creativity hemmed in by a well-modulated decorum that defies a bold splash of color? God invites us to bring our whole creative self to the altar and the adventure of faith. The Vatican II Council wrote these words of encouragement to artists: "This world in which we live needs beauty in order not to sink into despair. Beauty, like truth, brings joy to the human heart and is that precious fruit which resists the erosion of time, which unites generations and enables them to be one in admiration!"[2] So—what about classes, practice space, exhibits, movies, videos, gospel rap, Taize, labyrinth, displays, and jazzercise to honor our sacred gifts and unite us in beauty?

One year after presenting the creativity seminar at

First UMC in Pasadena, several ideas that were already percolating overflowed into a monthly exhibit of members' talents. The first year of displays featured a variety of talent, including needlework, fine woodworking, jewelry, watercolors, oil paintings, photography, gourds, dolls, and more. A carpenter was inspired to make moveable panels for the displays that are seen before and after worship. An artist statement and resumé tells the artist's story, while flowers and refreshments create an atmosphere of hospitality. These monthly exhibits and sales are anticipated by the congregation and artists alike who often combine their talents for the two-week exhibit.

The children's annual art camp has a display venue and is now linked to an outlet for the adults. Creativity as a vehicle to the community? A method of evangelistic outreach? Absolutely! The beauty of following your bliss is that the bounty touches other people and outruns your fondest dreams.

The beauty of following your bliss is that the bounty touches other people.

Creativity and stewardship? Of course! Another church uses creative gifts as part of its annual stewardship program. Each member is given ten dollars and required to bring it back threefold after three months of investing it with their talent. Jesus' parable of the talents in Matthew 25 is the biblical motivation for the program. Each Sunday is transformed into a "stewardship mall" where handcrafted items, food, recipes, calligraphy, silhouettes, seeds, plants, redeemable coupons, and you-name-it ideas line the tables of the fellowship hall and patio as members practice the parable of the two stewards (servants [NIV]) who invested their "talent" and were faithful.

A New Mission Statement

A statement of mission or purpose has become a necessity for any organization that takes its constituency and its future seriously. This is true for the business and corporate world, as well as for the church. This statement defines the calling, setting, and identity of a congregation and guides its course. It is often given a prominent place on the worship bulletin where it is seen on a regular basis. Sometimes these well-crafted statements are kept in a file drawer where they gather dust until the next year's planning retreat when they are reviewed and re-adopted with a few minor changes. Nonetheless they have the potential to breathe new life into every corner of the church's ministry, giving direction and unity to the many activities of the church as it relates to the community around it. Perhaps this is the time for your church to include a statement about the use of creative gifts in your statement of mission.

Many people in our churches spend full working days in creative pursuits in their jobs and in other ways, but do not have a sense that this is the work of Jesus. It is simply "what I do to make a living." We have little sense that work itself is sacred or that our gifts are holy.

The late Bishop Oscar Arnulfo Romero of El Salvador, a prophet in our time, embraced the sacredness of our daily actions when he wrote:

> How beautiful will be the day when all the baptized understand that their work, their job, is a priestly work, that just as I celebrate mass at this altar, so each carpenter celebrates Mass at the workbench, and each metalworker, each professional, each doctor with the scalpel, the market woman at her stand, is performing

130

a priestly office! Cabdrivers listening on your radio—
you are a priest at the wheel, my friend, if you work
with honesty, consecrating that taxi of yours to God,
bearing a message of peace and love to the passengers
who ride in your cab.[3]

Our eternal life is also our eternal creative life, and the
one is not separated from the other. "Born again" means
our gifts are born again also. They are not left out of the
equation. It is not enough to announce that Ms. Smith
likes to quilt or ride a bike, or that Joe Brown spends his
leisure time sailing or tutoring fifth graders. These creative outlets must be baptized into our discipleship and
devotion to Christ and his church. Somehow we think
that the church will intuit this truth. But it doesn't. We
see by the way creativity is relegated to a small area of
ministry that we don't get it yet.

The notion that we are given new life, eternal life,
through baptism somehow skips over our gifts. We are
asked to pledge our time, talents, giving, to Christ; but
our creativity is either assumed to be included or
assumed to be excluded. In any case, our creative gifts
and endeavors need a kind of blessing to be fully
included in the new life experience of living for Christ
in all we do.

No More Competition of Gifts

The path of our creative gifts should work its way
through the tasks of the church trustees to the preschool, into the choir cantata, to the homeless ministry, to the Capitol steps, and much farther beyond,
showing us the diversity and equality of talents that
God has given the church. These gifts have the power

to reach others, to spread God's good news, to discover our childlike nature, and to witness to God's love. The issues we face in our communities and the world are of such magnitude that we can no longer afford to separate our gifts and skills into disparate camps that cultivate one group's gifts while neglecting another's.

The shared ministry of clergy and laity is firmly rooted in our biblical and denominational history, a partnership we embrace in many ways. And yet the gift of creativity seems hidden from our eyes when we study the Scripture. Just as we read the Bible with an eye to finding young people, women, justice, cross-cultural issues, we can also read with an eye toward creative gifts beyond the "official list."

Art From the Heart

Creativity, or art, like the root word for liturgy, is also the work of the people, the *laos*, who receive God's gifts of imagination from the same generous heart that offers mercy, forgiveness, and grace. Our well-being is enhanced by creativity, revealing to us who God is. Its expression is more than an antidote for the blues or depression; it is critical to our experience of who God is. Incorporating it into the total life of our church as we worship, socialize, and serve is a witness to the heart of God that is our heart too.

We in the church might adapt the insight of Joe Khatena, author of *The Creatively Gifted Child: Suggestions for Parents and Teachers,* to recover our capacity to elevate the creative gifts of our community, thus blessing artists of all kinds in our congregations, affirming the spiritual dimension of creativity, and developing it in our children at an early age. "You have it in your power to cause creativity to happen and flourish before your very eyes. Be the catalyst of the mystery and magic of existence, for in the creativity of your child may lie a magnificent future for all."[4]

Corita Kent quotes the motto of the art department at Immaculate Heart College, which comes from the Balinese: "We have no art, we do everything as well as we can." The vocabulary of Balinese culture does not include the noun *art.* Their guiding philosophy is expressed in active verbs: "to dance, to sing, to paint, to play."[5]

In communities and countries where traditional ways of the elders, chiefs, and native inhabitants are still practiced, art is not a commodity that is produced, owned, and sold by a few talented people. It is the work of all the people. Likewise, in many African languages there is no word for art, although there are many words that indicate artistry; words like *embellished, decorated, beautified, out of the ordinary;* words that describe the skill, know-how, and inherent characteristics, something made by hand.

Our well-being is enhanced by creativity, revealing to us who God is.

We can certainly grow in the Christian faith without God's creativity; but when it is done with an eye to creativity, we retain our faith teachings longer and apply them to our lives more liberally. Research shows that lasting growth happens when we involve our whole selves in learning, relating it to our own lives. We can study faith in the traditional way—reading, lecturing, preaching, and discussion, service, mission—and we'll make laudable progress. We can use the same methods of learning with creative tools and

133

make quantum leaps in living it with our heart and our mind.

Reflections and Activities

1. Name the ministries of your church where creativity is evident. Are these the "predictable" places? Are there any surprises?

2. Make a list of the persons in the congregation who are known to be creative. How does each approach creativity? Do they ever work together? How might this group be expanded?

3. Take some time to re-read the mission statement of your church. Does creativity have a place in your statement? Could it be included? Whom do you need to talk to about this?

4. Is your church ready to "commission" the creative outlets of some of your members with the ritual in Appendix III on page 154? Perhaps a small group or ministry area might do this at a special gathering.

5. Take it as your holy assignment to begin a short-term study group on creativity as a divine gift. Assign readings and use the Bible generously. Publish your efforts and results in your church newsletter.

6. Make a group list of at least "25 ways to love your church—creatively" (see some suggestions in Appendix VII on page 164).

CHAPTER 10

You Can Get There From Here

When I changed my name almost twenty-five years ago I discovered that the distance from the A of Anderson to the S of Shamana is more than just nineteen letters of the alphabet. When we determine to make a creative change we often find it to be bigger than we anticipated. After living with a "personalized" name for so many years I still find new depths and definitions of what it means to me, to others, and new ways I can still grow into it.

What's in a Name?

Does changing our name count as a creative act? Nita Leland, artist and author, writes, "A creative act is not necessarily something that has *never* been done; it is something *you* have never done."[1] It counts. From marriage vows that result in a new family name to choosing a business name, a new name in a religious order, a name that expresses a cultural heritage, to the choice of a professional name, this is a critically important act that announces who we are to ourselves and to the larger community. Changing any part of our name is usually entered into with great intent and seriousness.

Sometimes our true name finds us even when we don't go searching for it. We humans have been known to give ourselves a new name that suits us more than the name we acquired at birth. We "fix" our names by abbreviating or respelling them for very personal reasons. Sometimes we are named by others for the qualities, physical traits, or habits and hopes they see in us, and the name sticks—and maybe we are drawn to live out its meaning.

When we consciously make creative decisions we don't usually do it with a chart of the creative process laid out in front of us. And yet we intuitively walk ourselves through each step of the process on the way to resolution. Let me suggest five steps of the creative process that have gained general agreement in the field.

Identification: Sometimes called First Insight, this first step is a statement of the problem, goal, intent of the process where we want to go. This phase can be said to use the right- and left-brain approach.

Saturation: The research phase, gathering as much data as possible, finding out what others have done; setting boundaries for the creative task, interviews, immersion in all relevant material at hand. This is the "L-Mode" or thinking stage of what we want to accomplish, when we develop sketches, make lists, and brainstorm ideas.

Incubation: The mulling over stage, letting it sit, putting it aside, leaving it alone so the unconscious mind can go to work on it. This stage requires a trust of the creative process—no hovering, no mothering. Incubation happens when our head is turned, while we're doing something else. Get out of the kitchen. Let the magic do its work.

136

Illumination: The solution comes, often as a sudden flash of insight, the "Aha!" moment; the "Eureka!" where we see the whole and all its parts. This stage reconciles and satisfies the "whole" brain. Sometimes the light comes as a distant glow that burns brighter and brighter as a solution is found. It is from this process that we learn creativity comes to the prepared mind.

Verification: Once the "Aha!" has occurred, there is a time of field testing feedback, confirmation, and checking for error and usefulness that completes the process.

Having identified these steps, let me now expand on them through my own experience of having changed my name.

Identifying the Problem—First Insight

A primary impetus for my own name change was to prepare for a new future in ministry and to remove the name taken in my former marriage, dissolved six years prior. The pressure of time and event provided a framework for this activity. I carried a mental picture of kneeling at the altar while the bishop laid his hands on my head, ordaining me to Christ's ministry with a new name, chosen for such a time as this. The seed of this possibility was planted shortly after arriving at seminary.

While attending a worship service nearby, I watched a mother and her adolescent daughter take new names in a very poignant ceremony. The daughter took the new name of Christ in a baptism service while her mother took back her parental family name after her divorce. There was great celebration for this family in the congregation, and the image of a new name was seeded in my imagination.

My immediate need was to begin ministry with a name that ushered me forward into the future to which God had called me. Unlike the renaming ceremony I had witnessed one year earlier, reclaiming my parental family name did not feel like a move toward the new future, although I treasured my family and the name I inherited at birth. Moreover, I wanted a name that was rooted in the earth and primal spirituality, a global name that transcended the boundaries of geography, custom, culture, even race, yet was intimately bound to these identities. The name would need to help me traverse the inner and outer journey of the spirit, reaching in while reaching out, bring healing and reconciliation, a name that meant seeing God in all things. This was to prove a tall order when starting from ground zero and facing a completion date a few months away.

Sometimes the statement of the problem or goal is the most important part of the creative process. The time spent in articulating this first insight phase can shorten the distance to illumination and yield great reward later as each phase of the creative process is initiated.

The Hunt Begins: Saturating the Brain

This phase of the process needs lots of input for the brain to work on so it can sort and sift, compare and contrast, intuit and image until it all comes together in the solution. In our Western culture we know how to do this phase well. We are trained to gather data, research facts, compile lists, and spout ideas. With a committed quartet of women friends at seminary we went to work on the saturation phase with a whirl-wind, L-Mode strategy. We fanned out and scoured books of names; first names, last names, English names, other language names; men's names; women's names; baby books; napkins; placemats; dictionaries; thesauruses; Bibles; telephone pages; garden books; libraries; bookstores; billboards; movie credits; family trees; and many, many, many, more sources. Oh, did I mention that the name had to be musical, have rhythm, several syllables, and a harmonious sound?

No pressure here. We checked in with each other regularly with sample bits and pieces of a suitable name. Nothing clicked yet. We kept saturating. Our shared task was done to cover as much ground as we could in as little time as possible. We had no intrinsic knowledge of the phases of the creative process, which is often the case when we proceed to solve a problem or gain first insight into a need. It helps to know that the first and fifth steps of the process fit more easily with our logical, analytical, research mode of operating, while the middle three phases draw on the more unconscious, subliminal side of our brain that responds to mystery and the numinous.

Into the Incubator

This is the hands-off phase. We've done all we can and it's now out of our control. We must stand aside. As much as we may need an answer to our insight within a certain time frame, the incubation phase can-not be hurried. It needs meandering time; brooding time; unhurried, unhassled time; unhooked from the tick of the clock, from deadlines, from schedules. This, of course is the ideal way. I had none of these creative

139

luxuries. I needed a name by June, preferably by May. Besides, I needed to send out notices of the change and arrive at the ordination service renamed and ready to be sent forth into ministry. This phase can be as short as the time it takes to walk to the kitchen and put on the coffee; or it can drag on for months, even years, before the answer emerges from our unconscious. It was now February. Come on, incubator.

Eureka! Illumination!

Fortunately, the birthing happened in an amazing and timely way. One April evening Penny called. "I've come across these concepts of ministry we studied in theology class today. Listen to this." Over the phone Penny read the paragraphs on how the minister embodies qualities of the shaman, the minister as mana-person, our connection to the ancient hunter-gatherer figure who brought divine healing and illumination to the people. As she spoke, my soul trembled. Fear and exhilaration danced in my mind simultaneously, the way the first steep climb of roller coaster cars coupled together produces both doubt and excitement as the peak of the tracks loom ahead. We know this is only the beginning of a long and thrilling ride and there is a lot to go through before it's over. "What do you think?" asked Penny. We played around with different combinations of words, spellings, pronunciations. Then we said *S h a m a n a* in tandem. Silence. More silence. "You know," I said, tentatively, "one of my strict requirements was that the name could not have any words of masculine derivation or meaning— *son, he, him, his,* or *man.* I want a female name. Now we have it twice, one word ending with *man,* the other

140

beginning with *man*." "Well," Penny answered, "maybe God's trying to tell you something. Besides, they're stuck in the middle." I was won over, with one caveat. "I'm going to make sure it's pronounced with a short 'a'; it sounds better like that anyway." Silence. More silence. "This is it! You have a new name!" "I have a new name!" We rejoiced together.

The revelation of the gift came not to me but to my friend. The divine route to resolution is not ours to program as we would like it to be. Neither can we guard the place where the answer will appear. We have been given to each other for much deeper revelations than we can possibly know. Sometimes we get a brief glimpse of the thin thread that weaves us into one family. Sometimes we can grasp the whole rope. When we do, it is an opportunity to praise God and to give thanks for the unity of the universe while we do our special part to maintain the thread called spirit.

The divine route to resolution is not ours to program as we would like it to be.

When Adam named the animals of the earth in the Creation story, I wonder if he touched every base of the creative process. Did *emu* emerge from the Incubation stage ? Was it in Saturation that *orangutan* was found? When did he ponder *giraffe* and *dinosaur*? Even when given a holy assignment, we cannot omit the partnership that continues with God.

That April night in Evanston my friends and I practiced rolling my new name around on our tongues many times, as Adam might have done with Eve over his charge to name the family of animals with whom we have kinship. I fell asleep with joy, with fear, and with trepidation, wondering what a new name would mean in the practical sense—changing forms, license,

141

Social Security, legal steps, informing people; all that stuff. We had been so focused on the content, we had yet to consider the portent. Beyond the practical matters I wondered if I had done the right thing. Was a name really that important? Would it be misunderstood in pronunciation? Would I be changed too? Somehow I knew that a giant step had been taken— but I could do no other.

The African American soul hymn, "Changed My Name," holds the key to my journey of the name and answers back to the promise of Jesus in Revelation 2:17: "I will give you a new name." With unrelenting poignancy, this plaintive melody weaves the soul of a people around the acceptance of a new name and a new life that overcomes hardships when lived in obedience to God through complete surrender and commitment to Jesus.

I told Jesus it would be all right,
   if He changed my name.
Jesus told me I would have to live humble,
   if He changed my name,
Jesus told me that the world would be against me,
   if He changed my name,
But I told Jesus it would be all right
   if He changed my name.

Verification

The verification stage began right away. Classmates and professors, record and financial offices were told that I had a new name. I was now "Shamana." I had moved from the beginning of the alphabet to the back of the bus. The response was generally receptive, but mixed with curiosity. The main question was "What does it mean?" Clearly it wasn't Smith, Brown, or Johnson to which most Americans relate. This was a name that didn't connect with anything we knew. We had no slot for it. How do you pronounce three *a*'s? Are they long *a*'s? Do they sound alike? Where is the accent? Is it really m - a - n - a, or should it be m - a - n — a, which we know how to pronounce even if itmakes for a funny name? Manna in the desert?

Maybe it sounds like the old rock-and-roll song that

Celebrating a New Name
Beverly Jean Shamana
(formerly Anderson)

*

𝔗𝔥𝔢 𝔍𝔬𝔲𝔯𝔫𝔢𝔶

A name is a significant symbol of who we are.

It brings with it history and heritage, and con-

tributes to the life and character of each of us. As in

the biblical Creation story, where naming expressed

the nature and God

relationship of the being so named, the naming

event is also embedded in those ancient roots. As I

celebrate the birth of this new surname, I also honor

the two names given at my birth and joyfully

embrace the totality of

my life's journey.

143

---

*

𝔐eanings, 𝔒rigins

Shaman: *One who illuminates and heals; raising the conscious-ness of the given community through images, myths, symbols, and metaphors of enlightenment. The Shaman bears the spirit of the Divine to humanity and embodies the powers rooted in the earth. The Shaman figure has origins in Eastern Asia and in the tribal cultures of Africa.*

Mana: *The divine essence and energy that is within us; a creative power greater than ourselves, which can be mediated but not totally possessed. Mana has origins in Oceanic or South Pacific cul-tures.*

---

starts out with "Sha-na-na-na, sha-na-na-na-na—Get a job . . . "? Verification was proving not to be so easy. For some, this phase is as simple as recording a for-mula, or writing out the tune that proves to be the answer to the creative process. It's over. It's done. Or it can take years of verifying the answer as a convinc-ing truth. Apparently mine was not going to be of the simple sort. So I prepared a notice of name change and mailed it to family and friends. It looked like this:

My goal of a name in time for the bishop's hand on my head at ordination was accomplished. Ministry colleagues were accepting and affirming. A serendipi-tous bit of verification came as we stood in the long line awaiting entrance onto the stage for presentation to the annual conference of The United Methodist Church. I rehearsed to an African American man in front of me the saga of formulating the name. When I turned around, a Korean man had apparently been lis-

144

tening to part of our conversation, so I pointed out that my name was changed for this occasion. His response, after reading my nametag: "Ah, yes. Strange name...Bee-verly." It worked! *Shamana* had currency on the international market. Turns out that *Beverly* is the unknown quantity in many circles. So be it.

The new name has a familiar sound to people from the Middle East, Asia, Africa, Spanish-speaking countries, young people of many cultures. I have been made honorary Japanese by many who assumed the spelling was *Shimada*, or *Shimoda*. I was even invited to preach based on the assumption that my name was of Japanese heritage.

A telephone operator in Telluride, Colorado helped me as I tried to register for a photo conference. As usual I was over-enunciating to distinguish between the *m* and the *n* so I wouldn't arrive to a nametag labeled as a mama. She cut to the chase, "Oh, you mean Mary - Apple - Nancy - Apple," she quipped. "Right," I said. (I'll take help wherever I can get it.)

Getting Beneath the Spelling

Sometimes there are holes in the whole that lead us to a new discovery. In my haste to put everything in place, I saved the cradle of my genesis until the end. Truth be told I was a little scared...and rightly so. The reluctance of my parents about this change in my life was predictable. They could understand the departure from my formerly married name, but why *Shamana*? To them it was weird, strange-sounding, unlike "regular" names. Foreign sounding. What is...a *Shamana*? My father was convinced it would

145

be a stumbling block to my ministry. "You won't be able to advance with a name like that," he said. Why not reclaim the family name. Was it so bad, after all? The new name became another step toward forming my identity and claiming the call to Christ's ministry as healing and reconciliation, a process that continues throughout our lives, as I continue to learn.

Nevertheless, as loving parents they made a valiant effort to understand my purpose and need for this new surname and gradually grew in their ability to say this new word to friends and family. Like a daughter who takes her husband's name, or partners with hyphenated names that require a jog in the memory each time it is said, over time my new name became a natural and accepted change to them. My three siblings accepted it more readily and sifted this new image into their ongoing picture of who I am. (I think.)

As hard as we worked during the winter quarter at seminary to choose the name within clearly articulated boundaries, the process required surrender to the Spirit and trust that God was in this search with us—not as a teacher standing at the front of the class who already knows the answer to a difficult question, but as a divine seeker with us, leading and looking throughout the earth for the name that would resonate with the person I was becoming. As hard as we tried, we could not squeeze an elegant combination of letters out of the known alphabet to compose the right word.

Letting God Choose for and Through You

Ultimately, I believe the name chose me. It came from a place I didn't know—through a channel beyond me—from a book and author I'd never seen, a theology book, an Episcopalian author, a friend's course work,

146

her connective mind. The name was looking for me as intensely as I was searching for it—another affirmation that we are God's vessels and partners, created to receive God's good pleasure and divine direction when we listen, declare ourselves open, and follow.

Since receiving my name I look for it in phone books when visiting other cities. I have yet to find another. There are often several *Shaman* and other similar sounding names. During my pastorate a church family chose it as their new baby's middle name, and I was privileged to perform the baptism. Some cultures use it as my first name. I have met young girls in their teens with similar first names—Shanna, Shama—but they stop short of the final two letters.

Almost twenty-five years after celebrating the name on the shores of Lake Michigan in the spring of the year with a dance of the scarves, naming liturgies, communion, gifts, and rituals with a quartet of like-minded seekers, the name that drew me into the future still presents a mystery to be plumbed. The depth of the name continues to call from the deep. I didn't know I was hovering near the mouth of the Shaman's cave until I started the journey to find a new name.

First Insight in the creative process may be only a glimpse of what we know to be true in the deepest recesses of our spirit.

First Insight in the creative process may be only a glimpse of what we know to be true in the deepest recesses of our spirit. I've learned that when a creative idea presents itself at your door it doesn't come across the threshold fully formed. Whatever part you can see, grab it—a foot, a finger, an ear—and keep pulling until the rest follows. You will be blessed.

147

The shaman is related to the role of the spiritual leader in a community. In *The Priest in Community*, Urban Holmes labels shamans "creatively weird, not just crazy, as it used to be common to think....[The shaman] must be...skilled in the receptive mode of processing experience....The [shaman, as the spiritual leader,] is called to illumine the people...[to call] up a world view for [the] people, [to create] images of order to heal a sense of chaos."[2]

I have now used over 3,700 words in this chapter to say that you are God's uniquely creative vessel of divine creativity and sacred spirit in the world. Perhaps you are beginning to let this truth seep into your cells and your bloodstream and the marrow of your bones. You have creative capacities that have been given to you that no one else has in quite the same way. You are special. You are creative. Believe it. Inhale it. Sleep it. Dream it. Sing it. Shout it! Draw it. Act it. Enfold it.

So what does this mean for you tomorrow? Next week? Next Christmas? It means that you can believe you are not imprisoned by what you are today. You can imagine another tomorrow that incorporates your creativity and go to work on it. A wise teacher once said, "The best time to plant a tree is twenty years ago. The second best time is today." So get out your shovel. Start digging. You are God's creative spirit. The world awaits your gifts! *Gloria in excelsis, Deo!*

Reflections and Activities

1. How do you feel about your name? What part of it would you change if you could? Who do you know

that has changed her or his name in an unusual way? Have you ever been called by another name? Share with your group the circumstances.

2. Keep a record of nudges or clues that might be "first insights" of a creative goal or problem.

3. Eighteen months after seeing the name change ceremony in worship, I initiated steps to change my name, although it had been brewing for six years. Is something simmering in your life that you want to make a creative change about? What is stopping you?

4. To really get under your own skin and find out what you really want to do, finish this statement: "If I weren't so scared, I would...." Complete it with ten answers. Write the statement again, then write ten more answers. Don't censor yourself. Write the first answers that come to your mind.

5. Name the ways others have hinted at your connection to mystery. Write the phrases, words, descriptions, conversations. Do these resonate with you? How?

6. Think about your usual way of taking in this external affirmation of God's spirit in you. Does it prompt a response in you? If so, what is it? What does it mean to you?

7. How will you start digging so that your creativity tree will flourish twenty years from now? What's your first step?

Appendix Overview

I. A Creativity Covenant

This covenant is just between you and God your Creator. Consider using it as a way to partner with God, to hold yourself accountable for cultivating the divine creative gifts within you, and to claim the love and support that God generously lavishes on your efforts.

II. Bliss 101

"Bliss 101: How to Fall in Love With Your Own Creative Gifts" offers a helpful checklist of new ways to think about what our gifts are. Perhaps you never thought about a particular skill or interest as a gift from God, but it is! Give yourself permission to enjoy.

III. A Service of Blessing for Artists and the Arts

Use or adapt this service of blessing after a creativity workshop, after completing the book and its reflections and activities, or within a worship service that recognizes the creativity that God has placed in all of us. In whatever setting you choose, this service will bring the worshipers into closer fellowship with God and each other as you strive to find your creative bliss.

IV. Creative Gifts 101

Use this article to give yourself permission to look for fresh insights into Scripture as a basis for your inherent creative gifts. A sample paraphrase of 1 Corinthians 12:4-26 will give you an idea of how to see anew how God may be speaking to you or how you may try your hand with another passage of Scripture.

V. Guided Meditation for Healing and Recovering Creative Power

This guided meditation can be used alone, with a partner, or with a small group. You may want to try it before you read the book. This visualization tool can help you become more aware of the supporting and discouraging influences that have affected your creativity and offer some healing.

VI. Creativity Tree

Use this visual image to identify and cultivate your own creative roots and recognize who nurtured you.

VII. Sixty Ways to Love Your Church "Creatively"

This list will help you spark and enjoy creative efforts in your various ministries and jumpstart our own brainstorming of more ways to be creative throughout the church.

VIII. Weekend Retreat Model

This sample model will guide you in preparing for a weekend retreat on creativity and spirituality.

Appendix I

A CREATIVITY COVENANT

I, *Your Name,* covenant with you, Creator God, to be open to nudges, clues, and messages from your Holy Spirit, to acknowledge your creative nature within me.

* I will be attentive to my interior landscape of dreams, memories, images, urges, and aches, that affirm my abilities and creative capacities.

* I will seek ways to relate to the natural and human world that make me aware of your active and divine creativity through others.

* I will engage in regular prayer, meditation, and holy conversations with others to nurture and support my current and emerging self-affirmation of creativity.

* I will actively take steps to release myself from past restrictions as I take bold new steps (and some baby steps) toward expanding my creative future. I will remember to give thanks to you.

Appendix II

BLISS 101
How To Fall in Love With Your Own Creative Gifts

1. Acknowledge the divine source of your creative being. (Don't fight it, just do it.)
2. Admit that you are powerless to excise this core of creativity from within you. (Accept it—you're made in God's image.)
3. Remember that you are free to use or ignore this power within you. (You still have free will.)
4. Our spirit yearns to express it. (Wake up and smell the watercolors.)
5. Travel in a group. We enjoy the ride much more when we connect with others who are on this journey. (Joy loves company.)
6. Make time to express yourself. (It is not wasted time; put it on the calendar.)
7. Acknowledge its significance for a healthy life. (It's not the icing, silly; it's the cake.)
8. Our creativity flourishes in the environment of affirming and supportive people in our lives—family, friends, colleagues. (Don't be a lone ranger.)
9. Creative expresion is a channel of divine revelation. (What a mystery!)
10. You have everything you need to get started. (Let go, you won't fall.)
11. Keep your day job. (You can be normal and creative too.)
12. Get a shovel and start planting your tree today. (Twenty years from now you'll be glad you did.)

Appendix III

A SERVICE OF BLESSING FOR ARTISTS AND THE ARTS

Gathering   *Family, friends, colleagues gather in the church, home, gallery, studio, or exhibit space.*

Greeting   *The pastor or leader addresses the gathering:*

Friends, we come together to acknowledge the honored place of the arts in the eyes of God. Early in the journey of the children of Israel, God named an artist to lead the Hebrew people in building the Tabernacle, God's home among the people. As we bless these persons who are called to a ministry of the arts, we honor the creative gifts that God has given each of them. We also acknowledge that each of us here has been blessed with creative abilities and talents; and we give thanks to God for the variety of creative gifts that bring us joy, that are a bridge to others, and that bring us closer to Christ.

Creativity is a natural part of being human. For the many ways we see its evidence around us, we are grateful. For these persons who engage in the arts as a primary vocation and for those who are responding to God's call in the creative arts, we bless them in this service that they may know the hand of God is upon their creative endeavors

Hymn of Thanksgiving
"Many Gifts"
"What Gift Shall We Bring"
or other music as appropriate

Scripture: Exodus 35:30-35—*Bezalel, the Artist*

Unison Prayer

Gracious and Loving God, who has shown us by your first acts of creation that we are made in your creative image, we honor you as the Supreme Artist.

Over the waters of Creation you mixed a palette of paints and brought forth a universe bathed in divine colors—heavenly hues that dazzle and delight our imagination. For this loving act that you called *"Good"* we give you thanks and praise. We rejoice with these persons who have heard your call to give themselves to the arts in a manner that honors your name. May they be so guided by your Spirit in their endeavors that all who are touched by their gifts will be drawn closer to your life-giving promise in Christ Jesus. We pledge our support of their gift even as we listen for your voice in the creative expression of our own talents from you. This is our prayer; in the name of Jesus Christ, our Lord. Amen.

A Litany of the Arts

Leader: We remember the beginning of the world when darkness covered the face of the deep and all things came into being with words, "In the beginning, God CREATED...."

People: Let us never forget our beginnings, the offspring of a creating God.

Leader: God of Bezalel and Oholiab, who quarried and cut stones, dyed and measured cloth, you show us how to use what is at hand to honor your name in artistic ways.

People: Show us the resources you have placed at our feet that none may be without a way to create.

Leader: God of sewing women and designing men,

People: Give us the courage to be creative in the face of opposition and status quo when you have shown us a new way for your sake.

Leader: God of creative children and talented youth,

People: Keep us mindful that talent is not bound by age and that we are mentors and models to those who follow after.

Leader: God of tired artists and those whose creativity is discouraged,

People: Surprise us again with creative inspiration in unexpected places.

Leader: God of Jeremiah, Isaiah, Amos, Miriam, and Huldah, who went to extremes as your prophets,

People: Free us to break out of our confining molds to stretch toward the potential you call us to.

Leader: God of healing, you touch our souls through creative art in ways that heal the wounds of the past. Free us to give and receive your creative gifts with new eyes.

People: Free us to see our wounds as gems of healing for ourselves and others.

Leader: God of mystery, who reveals precious things in the beauty of darkness,

People: Teach us to welcome the dark as a place of gestation, inspiration, and new birth.

Leader: God of our tribal and ancient ancestry, the Ashante, the Objibwe, the Mauri, the Seneca, and other tribal peoples, whose name we remember [*speak names here*], those who speak our names in other languages and other places with creative encouragement from the cloud of witnesses,

People: Give us wisdom to receive the benefit of their struggles and triumphs, failings and fears, that we may learn from their ways for the sake of the future.

All: God of all peoples, here and everywhere, whom you have gifted with unique and breathtaking creativity, grant that we may use creative art: the joining and the fitting together of things in new ways to shape a world that honors the gifts of each person, that we may live in harmony and give glory to your name.

Dedication

Where laying on of hands or kneeling at the altar is appropriate, the following may be offered:

Name(s), we dedicate you to the ministry of the arts, especially the art of _____. We confirm God's creative Spirit within you for the expression of this creativity to the honor of God's Name. **Amen.**

Applause, music, and other expressions of affirmation are invited.

Giving of Certificates or Other Mementos

Closing: From Bezalel's Commission

"See, [the LORD has] called by name Bezalel son of Uri son of Hur.... [God has] filled him with divine spirit, with ability, intelligence, and knowledge in every kind of craft, to devise artistic designs." Let us go forth to be good stewards and encourage this divine gift within us. Amen.

Adjourn to exhibit, celebration, fellowship, refreshments.

Appendix IV

CREATIVE GIFTS 101

Creativity, like laughter, is a natural human expression. It just happens if we let it. With this in mind, while driving to a church to lead a Lenten study on Faith and the Arts, I decided to use the familiar spiritual gifts passage in 1 Corinthians 12:4-26 to expand the image of our gifts. I asked the group to fill in the blanks using their own gifts, as I read aloud this familiar passage.

If you know this list well you will see a different side of it; and if you have not yet found yourself in Paul's summary, I offer our study group's creative rewrite from the third week of Lent.

We had fun with the Scripture by connecting it to our creative gifts while gaining insight into its meaning. Who says we have to read it just as it's written? Over the years many contemporary adaptations have won the hearts of preachers and congregations alike. God is creative, with a sense of humor too, and 1 Corinthians 12 is now planted in our hearts to remind us of our friends and the many ways we are blessed by their variety of creative gifts. You may want to compose a "new" Chapter 12 for your church.

A "New" 1 Corinthians 12:4-26

There is a variety of gifts, but always the same Spirit. There is a variety of ministries, but we serve the same One. There is a variety of outcomes, but the

158

same God is working in all of them. "To each is given the manifestations of the Spirit for the common good."

To one the Spirit gives wisdom in **storytelling**, to another, the words of **writing,** through the same Spirit. Through the Spirit, one person receives knowledge of **woodworking;** through the same Spirit, another is given the ability to **teach children,** and still another, power to **dance. Art** is given to one, to another, power to make things **grow.** One receives the gift of **sewing**, another, **mechanical knowledge.** But it is the one and same Spirit who produces all these gifts and distributes them as the Spirit wills.

If the **cook** should say, "Because I am not a **musician,** I do not belong to the body," does that make **cooking** any less a part of the body? If the **technician** should say, "Because I am not an **orator,** I do not belong to the body," that would not make it less a part of the body. If the body were all **orators**, what would happen to the **technicians?** If all were **technicians**, what would happen to our sense of **gardening**? Instead of that, God put all the different parts into one body on purpose. If all the parts were alike, where would the body be?

There are indeed, many different members but one body. The **inventor** cannot say to the **singer**, "I do not need you," any more than the **storyteller** can say to the **cook,** "I do not need you." And even those members of the body that seem less important are in fact indispensable. We honor the members we consider less honorable by clothing them with greater care, thus bestowing on the less presentable a propriety which the more presentable do not need. God has so constructed the body as to give greater honor to the lowly members, that there may be no dissension in

159

the body, but that all the members may be concerned for one another. If one member suffers, all the members suffer with her, if one member is honored, all the members share his joy. You, then are the body of Christ, and each of you is a member of it.

Gloria in Excelsis, Deo.

Appendix V

GUIDED MEDITATION FOR HEALING AND RECOVERING CREATIVE POWER

Preparation

Find a comfortable place to sit—in a chair or on the floor. Remove everything from your hands or lap. Let your body relax. Close your eyes. Inhale deeply through your nose, and exhale through the mouth as the leader gives instruction.

Meditation

Read this meditation slowly, to yourself or aloud with a group. Pause after each sentence or two to allow time to steep yourself in the image. Do not rush; enjoy the sensations and visual imagery that this meditation will create in your mind's eye.

Allow yourself to begin a journey. You are walking along a lovely path that leads to a place that is very special to you. Look around you. This place is filled with the things that you love. What are the colors, terrain, time of day, smell, weather? Just enjoy the surroundings that make you feel good. Take them into your being. These are God's gifts to you whom God loves.

As you are enjoying this beautiful place, you see a person in the distance who is approaching you. As the person gets closer, you can see that it is someone who has encouraged you in your creative endeavors. Greet this person. In your mind's eye, see the inner beauty of this person who has had such faith and belief in your potential. Tell this person what you have done or would like to do because of that trust in your capacity. Recall a special time when the trust and encouragement of that person meant a lot to you. Stay there until it feels right to part company. Thank this person and say goodbye.

As you watch this person move away, you see another person approaching. They pass each other as one leaves and the other draws nearer. You see that this second person is one who did not encourage your creative abilities. This is the person who withheld appreciation or was not able to see your creative talent or perhaps redirected your gifts in a less creative direction. Greet this person. Likewise, tell this person what you have done or would like to do with your creative ability. Say whatever else you need to say to this person. Take a moment to look deeply inside this person as you try to understand what motivated the lack of support you felt. If you are able, tell this person what you need now. If forgiveness is what's needed, give it. Receive divine reconciliation for yourself and for this person. Depart in a way that has meaning for you.

Closing

You are now alone. Mark this place with a symbol of this special meeting. You are now going to return from this place. Moving at your own pace, begin to mentally move back to the space where you began. Notice that you feel a release from any burden you have carried about your creative abilities. When you are ready, write about this experience or share with a trusted friend.

Appendix VI

THE CREATIVITY TREE

Appendix VII

SIXTY WAYS TO LOVE YOUR CHURCH "CREATIVELY"

1. Offer prayers of repentance for neglecting creativity in the past.
2. Write or use the "Litany of the Arts" for creative gifts in the church and community (page 155).
3. Hold creative gifts days.
4. Honor the workers in Matthew 25, and probe the mind of the third worker who buried his talent.
5. Lift up Bezalel and Oholiab as artists with creative vocation in the Bible.
6. Create a bibliography for further study of creativity and faith.
7. Invite guests to speak about their creativity and their faith.
8. Hold a children's art exhibit with a special display in nicely decorated rooms with matted and framed work. Serve refreshments, play music, and make artist brochures.
9. Recognize creativity in different areas of life.
10. Hold a talent dollar project.
11. Do a survey of talents.
12. Publicize community creative events and attend as a group.
13. Invite people inside and outside the church to give lessons in their creative expertise.
14. Hold monthly exhibits in the church hall after worship. Make nice bio sheets.

15. Publicize in the community newspaper.
16. Use more color in the church.
17. Hold a men's creativity day.
18. Do the same for youth.
19. And women.
20. And children.
21. Invite music teachers to hold recitals at your church.
22. Have pianos tuned.
23. Make videotapes of creative events.
24. Have a day to exchange creative "stuff" you no longer want or have room for.
25. Put up posters and signs that encourage creative expression.
26. Remind people frequently that God loves art.
27. Put on plays.
28. Use drama in worship.
29. And dance too.
30. Bring in drama and dance teachers for adults and youth and children.
31. Sponsor your pastors and worship leaders to attend creative workshops.
32. Use your children's art for bulletin covers.
33. Hold art camps or combine with another church for expanded arts and camping opportunities.
34. Learn body sculpting for making the Bible come alive.
35. Use humor a lot.
36. Study biblical dreams.
37. Make collages of your dreams in a group setting.
38. Make masks and wear them; combine with Scripture on "Love your neighbor as yourself."
39. Learn another culture's art.
40. Become pen pals.
41. Write your life story and share it.

42. Collect poems and stories and publish them through the church.
43. Publish a devotional book of seasonal meditations from members.
44. Celebrate Saint Francis: hold a pet blessing day and include prayers for pets that have died.
45. Make a giant group mural for a church room with the help of a muralist.
46. Plant a church garden and use the food for church dinners and for local food pantries.
47. Bake the Communion bread.
48. Make a stole with a special theme for the pastor.
49. Make a set of banners for the sanctuary.
50. Recognize members' cultural background with food, music, clothes, dance, social concerns, and needs.
51. Teach pottery classes—God is a potter (see Isaiah 64:8).
52. Teach a second language to English-speaking folks.
53. Walk a labyrinth.
54. Teach cooking.
55. Explore deaf ministry.
56. Recruit professional artists to use your church for rehearsal and performance.
57. Hold a walking tour of interesting places in your city.
58. Create a Web site for your church.
59. Start a voice choir.
60. Encourage men and boys to develop their creativity, then applaud it.

Appendix VIII

WEEKEND RETREAT MODEL

Purpose: To discover and celebrate God's creativity within us.
Maximum participants: 20
Suggested Time: Friday evening to Sunday noon

What Participants Bring

✸ Study book: SEEING IN THE DARK
✸ Bible of your choice
✸ Camera
✸ Small notebook for keeping a journal, notes
✸ One or two items that are "sacred" for you
✸ Two old magazines and photos for collage making
✸ One or two photos of yourself for collage making
✸ Pen, favorite color marker
✸ Scissors
✸ One candle and holder
✸ Personal items as needed

What the Leader Brings

✸ Box of crayons for each participant
✸ Extra magazines
✸ White glue, glue sticks
✸ 30 sheets of 8½-by-11 unlined paper and 11-by-17 white paper for collage background, or lightweight posterboard to be cut in various sizes
✸ Miscellaneous items for Sankofa bridge: string, tape, paper clips, transparent tape, colored paper, straws, yarn, popsicle sticks, ribbon, etc.

✳ Fabric or scarves for altar adornment
✳ Masking tape for display
✳ Felt-tip pens for outlining parts of collage
✳ Copies of hymns "Open My Eyes That I May See" and "Morning Has Broken" for each person
✳ One package of specialty paper with interesting background for poetry
✳ A small inexpensive memento of the retreat from leader for each participant
✳ Nametags
✳ Tape recorder or CD player and soft music

What to Do Before You Arrive
✳ Read the study book.
✳ Read Exodus 35:30-36.
✳ Interview three co-workers or members of your congregation about their creative outlets; how often and when do they feel creative? What inspires them? Is their faith involved in their creativity? What happens when they ignore their creativity?

FRIDAY EVENING

GETTING ACQUAINTED (*1 hour*)
Growing a Tree
As people arrive give each a nametag and invite them to make a distinctive nametag that is special for them. Welcome the group and invite all persons to share their name and the name and relationship of the person who first recognized or encouraged their creativity. Only the two names should be given as more time will be available later for more detail.

Share purpose of the weekend by reading Chapter 1, pages 11 and 12 (to "The 'Divine Spark' "). Teach the

168

song: "God Is Moving Among Us" (page 178). Sing two stanzas and two choruses. Ask the group to create another stanza to express God's creativity within them.

Gathering Prayer *(everyone)*
Gracious God, who created all things and called them good, we give thanks that you are a creative and creating God in whose image we are made. We joyfully place ourselves in your hands, trusting that our creative gifts and talents, used and unused, will flourish and be enriched as we offer them to you.

We open ourselves to the leading of your Spirit within and among us, knowing that you desire the highest good for us. We believe that our creativity is a part of the abundant life that your son Jesus came to earth to bring.

Show us the deeper meaning of your spirit in us that we may gladly bear witness to your love through the expression of our creative gifts. We dedicate this time to you that it may be a blessing to us and to others; in Jesus' name we pray. Amen.

Celebrate Encouragers
Invite group members to talk for three to four minutes each about the person who saw and nurtured the creative spark in them. (If the group is larger than twelve, do this in small groups of three or four.) Have each person (or one from each small group) share one "pearl" (not the whole oyster, please).

Read together the words of Dorie Ellzey's song, "The Ones Who've Gone Before Us," on page 25. Each person will then write the name of the encourager into the roots of the Creativity Tree and offer a silent prayer of thanksgiving. (See page 163 for the tree.)

CLAIMING OUR CREATIVE FUTURE *(1 hour)*

A Collage

After all instructions are given, this activity should be done in silence so persons can create a tiny bubble and communicate with God, their design, and themselves.

Give each person a box of crayons. Ask each participant to take out her or his favorite color; hold it in his or her hand; smell it; peel it; then break it, reminding them of the "aura" that surrounds tools of creativity. Crayons may be used in the collage. This activity will begin to identify creative blocks, barriers, and growth areas.

Spread magazines on tables; distribute scissors and glue. Use 11-by-17 sheets of paper or cut poster paper into smaller sizes. Use scissors and/or tear magazine pictures or parts of pictures to select images that represent your creative future or affirm your present creativity. Glue with overlapping edges. Outline with felt-tip markers as needed. Include photos of yourself. If you finish early, go back to the Creativity Tree and fill in the "roots" with names of family and friends in your past who were known to be creative. Begin to color the tree. Give your artwork a title and date and sign your work. Write the name and relationship of your creativity encourager on a sheet of paper to be displayed next to your collage.

Find a place to display the artwork on flat surfaces or tape to walls where permissible.

Silent Gallery Walk

When all have finished or an hour has passed, have a gallery walk to view all the designs. Let the work speak for itself. If time and energy permit, participants may comment on each other's work with words of appreciation, observations of mood, tone, color, line, surprise, about the collages. Express thanksgiving for all the work.

Closing Blessing

Select someone to read The Chinook Blessing on page 29. Have the group join hands and sing "God Is Moving Among Us," page 178.

SATURDAY MORNING

GATHERING *(10 minutes)*

Sing

Sing together "Open My Eyes That I May See."

Pray

Lead group in morning prayer together:

God of the morning, God of the night, God of the artist within, we praise you for the gift of life that surrounds and upholds us. We who are made in your divine image give thanks for your creative life that flows through us and all creation. Guide us by your Spirit as we greet this new day. Touch us with your creative hand that we may reflect your gifts in us and give honor to your name. We trust the One who is in our midst, the Spirit of Christ who enables our doing and making, our joining and fitting, as artists and creators of life. Amen.

REPRISE *(45–60 minutes)*

Complete Gallery Walk

Complete "Gallery Walk" questions not finished from the night before. If some artists want to comment on their own work or process, now is the time.

Check on Dreams

Check in for night dreams that some may want to include in their collage with a dream image.

"Haiku"

This activity will close or contain the collage. Each person will write a three-line haiku, Japanese-style poem that describes his or her experience of the collage process. (The first line has five syllables, the second has seven, and the third has one syllable; but you needn't be rigid.) After fifteen minutes, each person will read her or his poetry. Repeat the circle again. Express appreciation to each other.

SANKOFA BRIDGE: WALKING WITH CREATIVE MENTORS AND MONSTERS *(1 hour)*

Read and review the Sankofa bridge, pages 18–20. Ask: What might a Sankofa or memory bridge look like? Why is it important?

Instructions: Form teams of four people other than those in the "get acquainted groups." Set out all bridge-building materials. Build a Sankofa bridge using whatever materials are at hand and any that your team can gather up in the retreat environment. You must be able to present a rationale for your Sankofa design. Check into Chapter 2 as you build so that it supports the principles of Sankofa. Time allotted for building—20 minutes.

Building Guidelines: The Sankofa bridge must support the weight of a pencil; it must have a "span"— not touching the table or floor underneath in its middle section; every team member must be involved.

Group Presentations: Each group will present and describe its bridge and why it was constructed in that manner. Display in work area.

Conclude with a Verse of "God Is 'Bridging' Among Us," page 178.

MORNING BREAK *(15 minutes)*

BEZALEL—GOD'S CREATIVE CONTRACTOR
(45–60 minutes)
Review Chapter 3 together. Look for unusual circumstances in the Tabernacle project as described in Exodus 35: Bezalel's role with Oholiab, his supervision of the people, how he was called to use his gifts for this building campaign. Review and discuss the "Reflections and Activities" (page 44) together.

Ask: Would our bridges have looked any different if Bezalel were supervising them? Was there a team effort in the Sankofa bridge building? Were any personal items used? What were the team roles as the bridge developed? Was this an R-Mode or L-Mode activity? (See chart on pages 67–68.) How did you celebrate your project? Was anything missing?

Sing together "This Little Light of Mine."

LUNCH

HANDS-ON CREATIVITY SESSION *(2½–3 hours)*
Begin the afternoon session with a centering journal entry. Play soft music in the background. Give each person pen and paper, or journal notebooks may be used. You will begin a statement and participants will complete the statement according to the category you give. Write in silence.

173

I am (*name an emotion*)_____
I am (*name a kind of music*)_____
I am (*name a color*)_____
I am (*name an element in nature*)_____
I am (*name one of the senses*)_____

Instruct the group in the art process being used in the creativity exercise: clay, wood, painting, gourds, shells, stones, fabric, and so on. Keep the project simple enough so that it can be completed in one afternoon. Participants should be able to take a finished piece of creativity home with them. This creative time should be done in as much silence as possible. It is a time to commune with God, with creativity, with self. Background music can be played. It should not intrude into the flow of creative juices.

FREE TIME (*at least 1½ hours*)

Allow at least one and one-half hours of free time before dinner for those who want it. Free time might include rest, walking, meditating, reading, writing in a journal on aspects of the Creativity Tree, pre-retreat interviews, insights arising from the weekend, vocational thoughts, considering how your church might grow in its creative efforts, or spending time with chapters and questions in the study book.

DINNER

DISCOVERY (*45 minutes*)
Guided Meditation
Prepare the group for this experience with the assurance that it is a gift that they may give themselves. Persons will discover more about themselves and

174

their creative blocks and openings and will be freed to use more of their creative gifts. Invite participants to find a comfortable space on the floor or in a chair. Follow the guided meditation script on page 161. Do remember to read slowly so the imagination has time to do its work within each person. Debrief the experience as the script suggests.

"Haiku"

Each person will compose another haiku poem. After fifteen minutes, each poem is read, twice around the group. After all have read, let the group affirm each other individually by saying: *"Name*, we bless you, we thank God and *name of first encourager* for you. Your creativity is a gift to the world."

NIGHT PRAYER *(5–10 minutes)*

Dear God: We thank you for the beauty of this day and for the gift of the night. Bless the hours of our rest. Continue your creative work in us through dreams and visions that affirm your gifts in us. Awaken us to greet another day with joy. We pray in the name of Him who is spirit and light, your supreme gift to us, Jesus Christ our Savior. Amen.

ASSIGNMENT FOR SUNDAY

Read Chapter 7, "Seeing in the Dark," to prepare for Sunday worship. Transfer both haiku poems to specialty paper, using felt-tip pens, crayons; sign and date. These will be used in worship.

SUNDAY MORNING

PREPARATION *(10–15 minutes)*

Sing together "Morning Has Broken."

Give worship assignments for preparation: design an altar using group candles, fabric, scarves. Prepare the room with bridges, collages, haiku. Reader for Scripture, for prayer, for consecration.

WORSHIP SERVICE

Song: "God Is Creative Within Me" (page 178)
Prayer
Scripture: Matthew 5:13-16 and 13:45

Group Sermon: "The Pearl of Christ Within Me"
Form new groups of four; share the creative pearl found glowing in the dark this weekend. After fifteen minutes, select one pearl to be shared with the whole group when it reassembles. One person from each group shares a pearl—up to three minutes each.

Song: Saint Patrick's prayer, sung to tune "Alleluia" (see page 104)

Affirmation of Creativity: See Appendix I, page 152
Group Reading and Signing of Covenant

Closing Song: "This Little Light of Mine"
1) Everywhere I go,
2) All around the world,
I'm gonna let it shine.

Closing Prayer: (*holding hands*)
Our Loving and Creating God,
Our hearts are filled to overflowing as we see how you have created us in your image and given us gifts beyond measure. For this time apart to give and receive, to forgive and be freed, to claim our creative

176

future, we give you praise and glory. We are grateful for the shoulders we stand on and for seeds of creativity planted before our birth. We go forth from this place holding in our hands the keys you have placed there that have unlocked our creativity. We use it as an act of worship to you, that it may bring us personal joy, and help make our world a better place for all. We thank you in the name of Jesus, your most holy gift to all creation. Amen.

Mementos From Leader: Give to each person with these words: "The world awaits your gift. Be bold for God."

God Is Moving Among Us

B. J. SHAMANA

1. God is mov-ing a-mong us. Sing al-le-lu___

ia. _____ ia. Sing al-le-lu-ia. Praise your

name, the God of heaven and earth pro-claim.

2. God is healing among us......
3. God is loving among us.......
4. Christ is calling within us.....
5. Spirit's dancing among us.....

Notes

Preface

1. Michael Polanyi, chemist-turned-philosopher; reference in *Ministry and Imagination*, by Urban Holmes; The Seabury Press, 1981; pages 106–107.
2. *The Artist's Way: A Spiritual Path to Higher Creativity*, by Julia Cameron; A Jeremy P. Tarcher/Putnam Book, 1992.

Chapter 1:

1. Quoted in *Walking on Water: Reflections on Faith and Art*, by Madeleine L'Engle; North Point Press, 1995; page 72.
2. Quoted in *The Psychology of Invention in the Mathematical Field*, by Jacques Hadamard; Dover, 1945.
3. Ivy Books, 1993.
4. *Centering in Pottery, Poetry, and the Person*; Wesleyan University Press, 1989; page 40.

Chapter 2:

1. Quoted in *A Kick in the Seat of the Pants: Using Your Explorer, Artist, Judge & Warrior to Be More Creative*, by Roger van Oech; Perennial Library, 1986.
2. Quoted in *Earth Prayers From Around the World: 365 Prayers, Poems, and Invocations for Honoring the Earth*, edited by Elizabeth Roberts and Elias Amidon; HarperSan Francisco, 1991; page 125.
3. Song copyrighted by Dorie Ellzey Blesoff © 1975. Song is available in songbook/tape collection entitled *No Way to Stop This Miracle*. Email address *dorieblesoff@hotmail.com*. Used by permission.
4. *Women Who Run With the Wolves: Myths and Stories of the Wild Woman Archetype*, by Clarissa Pinkola Estés, Ballantine Books, 1992; "The Sixth Task."
5. "Artist Statement," December 1995. Used by permission.
6. *A Kick in the Seat of the Pants*; page 138.
7. *The Wounded Healer: Ministry in Contemporary Society*, by Henri Nouwen; Image Books, 1979; page 96.
8. Quoted in *Earth Prayers*, page 107.

Chapter 3:

1. *Wishful Thinking: A Seeker's ABC*, by Frederick Buechner; HarperSan Francisco, 1993; page 119.
2. *Wishful Thinking*, page 118.
3. *Learning by Heart*, by Jan Steward and Corita Kent, Bantam Books, 1992; page 5.
4. *State of the Arts: From Bezalel to Mapplethorpe*, by Gene Edward Veith, Jr.; Crossway Books, 1991; page 111.
5. *Learning by Heart*, page 71.

Chapter 4:

1. *The Courage to Create*, by Rollo May; Bantam Books, 1985; pages 44–45.
2. *Centering in Pottery, Poetry, and the Person*; page 40.
3. *Drawing on the Right Side of the Brain*, by Betty Edwards; Simon and Schuster, 1979; page vi.
4. *The Courage to Create*; page 49.
5. *Voicing Creation's Praise: Towards a Theology of the Arts*, by Jeremy Begbie; T&T Clark, 1991; page 228.
6. *The Courage to Create*; page 49.

Chapter 5:

1. "Always Two Steps Ahead," by Katherine Fulton, in *Los Angeles Times Magazine*, October 30, 1994; page 40.
2. Interview, used by permission of Minnietta Millard.
3. *Spirit in the World*, by Karl Rahner; Herder and Herder, New York, 1968.
4. *Ministry and Imagination*, by Urban T. Holmes III; The Seabury Press, 1981; page 107.
5. *The Spirit of Synergy: God's Power and You*, by L. Robert Keck; Abingdon Press, 1978; page 88.
6. Ibid.
7. Used by permission of Dr. Betty Edwards.
8. *Drawing on the Artist Within*, by Betty Edwards; Simon and Schuster, 1986; page 6.
9. See "Notes: Preface, 2.," page 179.

Chapter 6:

1. Used by permission of Nora King.
2. *The Art Spirit*, by Robert Henri;

Harper & Row, 1951; page 15.

3. *Walking on Water*, page 23.

4. Used by permission of Minnietta Millard.

5. *Learning by Heart*, page 5.

6. The NAMES Project Foundation; *www.aidsquilt.org*.

7. *The Go-Between God: The Holy Spirit and the Christian Mission*, by John V. Taylor; Oxford University Press, 1979; page 19.

8. *The Courage to Create*, page 2.

9. Used by permission of Rhea Zakich.

Chapter 7:

1. Quoted in *A Guide to Prayer for Ministers and Other Servants*, by Reuben P. Job and Noman Shawchuck; The Upper Room, 1983; page 310.

2. *In the Minister's Workshop*, by Halford E. Luccock; Abingdon Press, 1944; page 108.

3. *Photography and the Art of Seeing*, by Freeman Patterson; Key Porter Books, 1985; page 9.

4. National Pulic Radio interview, April 8, 2000.

5. *Zen Seeing, Zen Drawing: Meditation in Action*, by Frederick Franck; Bantam Books, 1993; page 34.

6. Quoted in *The Creative Spirit*, by Daniel Goleman, Paul Kaufman, Michael Ray; A Plume Book, 1993; page 20.

Chapter 8:

1. "On Three Ways of Writing for Children," *Of Other Words: Essays and Stories*, edited by Walter Hooper; quoted in *Past Watchful Dragons*; Collier Books, 1979; page 1.

2. *Past Watchful Dragons*, page ix.

3. *Alo'ha-Ha-Ha: Recycled Jokes in Paradise*, by Alex Vergara.

4. Used by permission. For whole poem contact Spirit Brush Arts, Reverend Donna Fado Ivery, fadoivery@aol.com.

5. "The World's Last Night," *The World's Last Night and Other Essays*; quoted in *Past Watchful Dragons*, page 40.

Chapter 9:

1. Ministry of the Arts' Vision Statement,Sisters of St. Joseph of LaGrange, IL. Ministry of the Arts Catalog: www.ministryofthearts.org. Used by permission of the Sisters of St. Joseph of

LaGrange.
2. "Message to Artists," from the fathers of Vatican II Council, quoted in *Sacred Arts Festival: The Arts in Church and Home*, brochure for event June 10-11, 2000, Pasadena, California.
3. Prayer of Archbishop Oscar Arnulfo Romero of El Salvador.
4.Vantage Press, 1978; quoted in Marilyn Ferguson's *Book of PragMagic*, adapted by Wim Coleman and Pat Perrin; Pocket Books, 1990; page 180.
5. *Learning by Heart*, page 6.

Chapter 10:
1. *The Creative Artist: A Fine Artist's Guide to Expanding Your Creativity and Achieving Your Artistic Potential*, by Nita Leland; North Light Books, 1990; page 22.
3. *The Priest in Community: Exploring the Roots of Ministry*, by Urban T. Holmes III; The Seabury Press; pages 79, 80, 94.